BATIK

Traditional Textiles of Indonesia

FROM THE RUDOLF SMEND & DONALD HARPER COLLECTIONS

Contributors

Inger McCabe Elliott

Annegret Haake

Donald Harper

Jonathan Hope

Brigitte Khan Majlis

Rudolf Smend

Antje Soléau

Haryani Winotosastro

Maria Wrońska-Friend

Captions

Maria Wrońska-Friend

TUTTLE Publishing

Tokyo | Rutland, Vermont | Singapore

Galerie Smend

Contents

Preface

Thanks to the Museum Tekstil in Jakarta, a new publication on batik is being launched.

In 2000, I published a catalogue entitled *Batik: Javanese and Sumatran Batiks from Courts and Palaces*. His Highness Sultan Hamengku Buwono X and his wife Queen Hamas were kind enough to travel all the way from Yogyakarta to Germany to officially open the exhibition at the Rautenstrauch-Joest Museum in Cologne.

In 2006, the Deutsches Textilmuseum (German Textile Museum) in Krefeld invited me to display batik from my collection. The occasion was to mark one hundred years since the very first batik exhibition ever held in Germany—in Krefeld—had taken place.

In June 2015, the Museum Tekstil in Jakarta celebrated the opening of an exhibition entitled *Highlights from the North Coast to Bimasakti*, which presented pieces from Brigitte Willach and my collections. The planning and preparation for this event led to this, my third catalogue.

The main reason for producing this catalogue is to give thanks to my teachers, partners and heroes of more than forty years, among them Bambang Oetoro, Ardiyanto, Gianto C. P., Go Tik Swan Hardjonagoro, Iwan Tirta, Pak Soemihardjo, the Winotosastro family, T. T. Soerjanto, Ibu Eiko A. Kusuma, Nian S. Djoemena and Ibu Sa'adiah Munir Djody.

In 2010, Mary Hunt Kahlenberg and Ruth Barnes published their magnum opus, *Five Centuries of Indonesian Textiles*. This book certainly set a high standard and was greatly welcomed by lovers of Indonesian textiles. A second highly important publication was published in 2014—*Sarong Kebaya* by Peter Lee. It would be difficult to find a better book In this specialist field than Lee's masterpiece, a result of many years of collecting and research.

My approach needed to be different. I asked long-standing friends and specialists in the field to share their initial encounter with batik and their thoughts on it. Not everyone I approached was prepared to go along with my idea, and I am very grateful to the eight international aficionados and scholars who did. In addition to their contributions, I wanted to illustrate the book with as many unpublished photographs as possible from the "good old days" or *tempo doeloe*. All of them had to be related to batik. Now I am proud to present family portraits and private photos of people who never expected to be published, not only because of their station in life but also because of their attire, in this case batik. Many of the photos were taken in Central Javanese studios. This area has been my favorite place from the beginning of my batik journey in the early 1970s.

The Museum Tekstil's exhibition concept meant it was now my task to show as many fine examples of Pesisir (north coast) batik as possible. It was King Rama V of Siam, no less, who began collecting batik in Java in 1871 during his three trips to Indonesia. At the time, he favored the studio of Mevrouw Jans above all other artists. A hundred years later, I was able to locate batik signed by Mrs Jans. Thanks to Donald Harper and visits to auctions and markets in the Netherlands, it is possible to present some of this great artist's work today.

The batik section of this book consists of three main parts that run consecutively: first, signed Dutch batik (*batik Belanda*) or, strictly speaking, Indische batik, sometimes referred to as Indo-European batik, made by Dutch people who had long settled in Indonesia or Eurasians of mixed Dutch and Asian (Javanese, Arab or Chinese) heritage in the Pekalongan area, dating from 1880 to ca. 1930; secondly, early unsigned batik from the Pesisir area of Java, stretching from Cirebon in the west to Lasem in the east; and, thirdly, fine examples of batik made by Chinese Peranakan, the descendants of Chinese immigrants, who were born in the Indonesian archipelago.

What all these pieces have in common is the high standard of their workmanship. This is why we want to offer a belated tribute to numerous people who remain largely unknown:

The entrepreneurs, mostly women, who successfully managed workshops, often employing more than a hundred workers.

The designers who were inventive and adventurous enough to create designs and develop color combinations.

The thousands of female batik workers skilled at drawing fine lines and small dots on cotton, often in not very comfortable working conditions.

The dyers who experimented with natural and plant dyes and, after the turn of the century, became acquainted with chemical dyes from Europe. Most of their recipes have been kept secret, and it is with good reason that their profession is referred to as "the dyer's art".

Last but definitely not least, we are indebted to the people who ordered batik from the entrepreneurs. The occasion was frequently a wedding, and it was quite common to have to wait a year for the order to be fulfilled. We are also thankful to all those who kept these treasures as heirlooms in their homes for many years despite economic and political upheavals.

It is these people—most of them anonymous—who merit our deep appreciation, admiration and gratitude. Without their persistence, good taste, patience and entrepreneurship, we would be unable to appreciate these treasures today. We owe it to them that, in 2009, UNESCO designated Indonesian batik Masterpiece of Oral and Intangible Heritage of Humanity. We bow our heads and say *terima kasih* for being able to enjoy these wonderful works of art today.

A short note will suffice on the form of the cloths and the material from which they are made. A sarong is approximately 200 cm long and 105 cm wide and is usually sewn at the ends into a tubular skirt. Traditional sarongs have a central decorative panel called a *kepala* or "head", which differs in pattern and most often color from the *badan* or main "body" of the cloth. The sarong is worn with the *kepala* either at center front or back. A longer version of the sarong is the *kain*, also called *kain panjang* or "long cloth", which is about 250 cm long and 105 cm wide. It is unsewn and is usually decorated with an all-over design although a half *kepala* may be positioned at each end of the cloth. All the batik textiles in this catalogue are made of cotton. Until about 1910, most, but not all batik was dyed using natural dyes.

In most cases, we do not know the names of the people in the photos. Should readers identify a family member or friend, the publishers would be grateful for further details.

The contributors agreed to publish their email addresses. Readers are welcome to contact them and share their own experiences and adventures in the field.

For most of the words written in *italic* in the captions, a brief explanation can be found in the Glossary on pages 168–9. The modern media will help readers obtain further information, if required.

I would like to express my sincere thanks to the editorial teams in both Cologne and Singapore as well as the curators of the Museum Tekstil in Jakarta.

Rudolf Smend
August 2015

Overleaf An outdoor market in Java, ca. 1890.

From the Rudolf Smend & Donald Harper Batik Collections

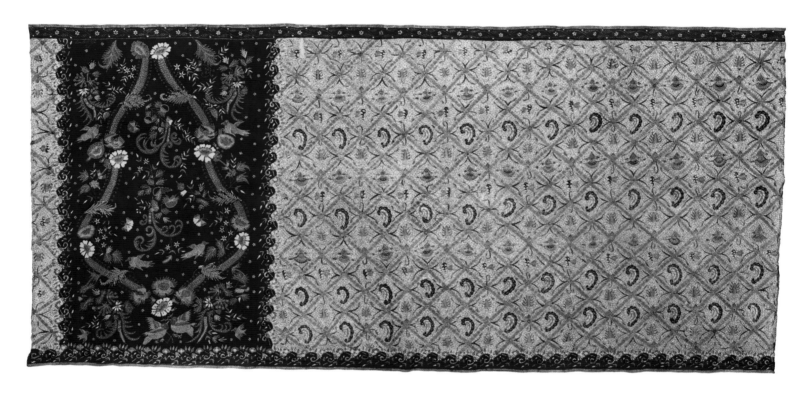

1 Sarong, signed "Mevr. B. Fißer Pek", Pekalongan, ca. 1880.

The batik workshop belonging to Mrs B. Fißer was one of the most famous in Pekalongan at the end of the 19th century. Mrs Fißer passed away in 1905. The decoration on this sarong combines Central Javanese motifs on the *badan* (main body) with Pesisir (north coast) motifs on the *kepala* (head). This hybrid style became popular in Pekalongan in the last years of the 19th century. The *badan* is decorated with *sidomukti*, a latticework composition containing symbols of prosperity and well-being, such as the wing (*lar*) of the mythical bird Garuda (seen also in the sarong on pages 72–3 and in the photos on pages 113, 135 and 137). In Central Java, *sidomukti* frequently features on batik worn by a bride and groom. On this sarong, the *kepala* is filled with garlands of flowers and pairs of lovebirds, which also make reference to a festive, joyful occasion. It is possible that this batik sarong was specially commissioned for a wedding.

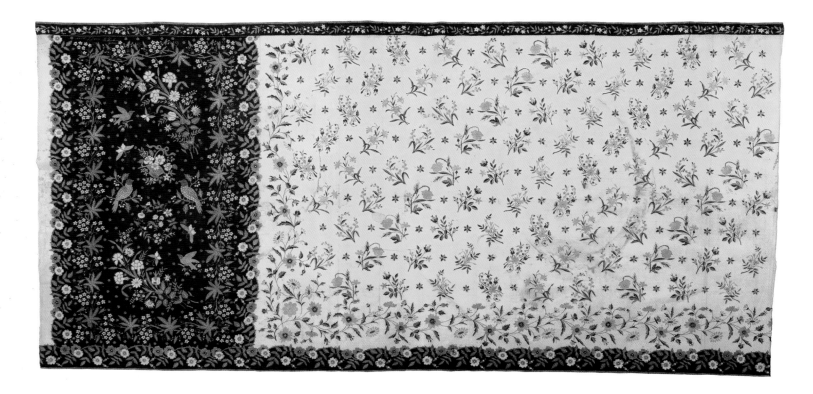

2 Sarong, signed "wed: J. Jans Pekalongan", made in Mrs J. Jans' workshop (ca. 1850–ca. 1920), ca. 1885–1900. The workshop of Mrs Jans catered to wealthy clients at the turn of the century, consistently producing batik with delicate scallop-like lacy borders and soft colors. This sarong depicts a range of dainty flowers favored by the Dutch residents of Indonesia, set against striking floral arrangements on a darker ground on the *kepala*. The *badan* has been decorated with rows of small bouquets of poppies, carnations, tiger lilies, forget-me-nots, lily of the valley and jasmine. To increase the dynamism of the composition, the rows of bouquets alternately slant left and right. The *kepala* features other very fine floral arrangements, such as a floating basket of flowers, two bouquets of mixed flowers and a round floral wreath, as well as butterflies in flight and birds perched on branches.

3 **Sarong kelengan, signed "wed: J. Jans Pekalongan", made in Mrs J. Jans' workshop (ca. 1850–ca. 1920), ca. 1885–1900.**
Among the Chinese Peranakan of the Pesisir area, blue and white batik (*kain kelengan*) used to be worn during a period of mourning. In some families, a bride would also wear a sarong with this range of colors to indicate her sorrow at leaving her parents' house. At the same time, a wedding was a joyful occasion, therefore on the *badan*, bouquets of lilies and Lenten roses are interspaced with floating baskets of flowers, birds and butterflies. On the *kepala*, the joyful atmosphere has been further enhanced with a centrally positioned bouquet of roses and baskets of carnations, surrounded by the graceful stems of jasmine.

4 **Sarong buketan, signed "J. Jans", made in Mrs J. Jans'**
  workshop (ca. 1850–ca. 1920), Pekalongan, probably
  after 1900.
  This sarong derives its name from the floral bouquets
  (*buketan*; *boeket* in Dutch) that are evenly arrayed along
  the *badan* and *kepala*, a tribute to the beauty of tiger lilies.
  Four elaborate bouquets of tiger lilies decorate the *badan*,
  while the same arrangement, presented as a mirror image,
  dominates the *kepala*.

5 Sarong, signed "wed Jans–Pekalongan", made in Mrs J. Jans' workshop (ca. 1850–ca. 1920), ca. 1885–1900.
This sarong has been dyed with typical colors of the Pesisir area—indigo blue, made from the leaves of the indigo plant (*Indigo tinctoria*), and a deep turkey red called *mengkudu*,

produced from the bark of the roots of *Morinda citrifolia*—with each color executed in at least two hues of varied intensity. The main feature of the *badan* is a garland of flowers that runs down each side of the *kepala* and along the lower edge of the cloth, while the background has been covered with hundreds of stylized jasmine flowers spaced at regular intervals. The *kepala* presents a large bouquet of Margaret flowers, a common species of daisy, and fuchsia.

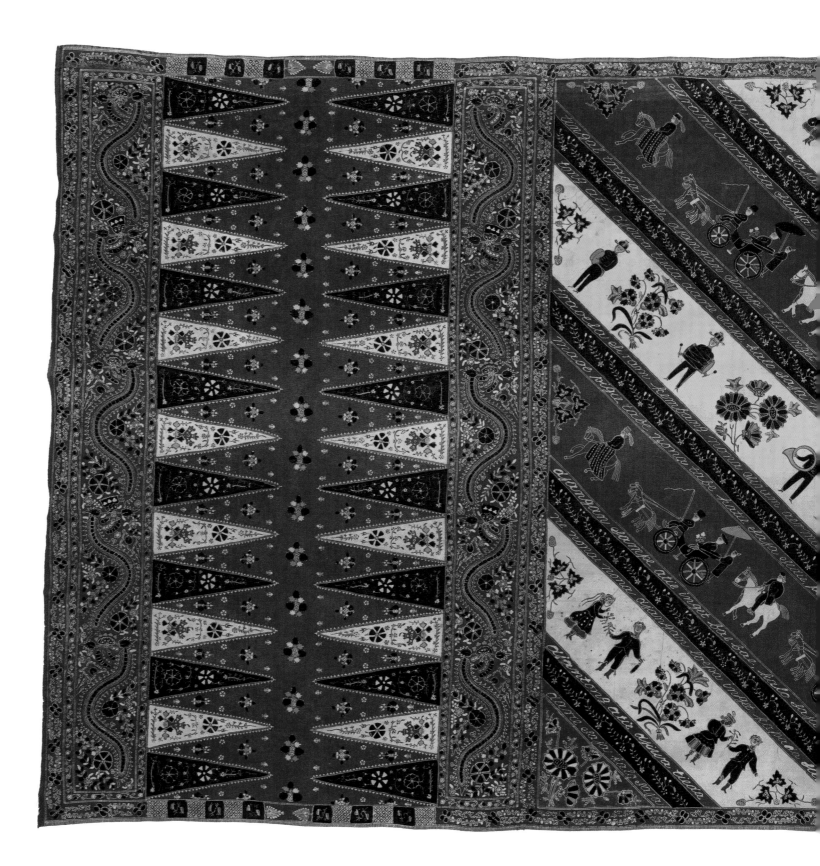

6 Sarong, Pesisir area, second half 19th century.
Around 1860, batik sarongs decorated with poems in the
Malay language became popular on the north coast of Java.
As this cloth indicates, the text and the iconography did not
always complement each other. The poem shown on this

sarong, written by a man (see the original and the translation on page 174), mentions a farewell and parting with a loved one, while the diagonal bands separating the lines of the poem feature romantic and happy scenes, suggestive of an engagement and marriage. The bands depict a man presenting flowers to a young woman and there is a large music band and horse-drawn carriages. Numerous bouquets of flowers enhance the celebratory atmosphere.

7 **Sarong, signed "Drinhuijzen Pek", made in the Drinhuijzen workshop, Pekalongan, 1890s.**
The Drinhuijzen workshop was active in the 1870s to 1890s.
On this sarong, scattered groups of cornflowers decorate
the *badan*, while the *kepala* features smaller blossoms on
a background covered with a multitude of tiny, stylized
jasmine blossoms.

8 Sarong dlorong buketan, signed Mrs "L. Metz Pek", made by Mrs Lien Metzelaar (ca. 1855–1930), Pekalongan, ca. 1890–1900.

Mrs Lien Metzelaar ran a well-known batik workshop in Pekalongan between 1880 and 1919, the heyday of Indische or Indo-European batik. She frequently signed her batik "L. Metz Pek". Between 1890 and 1900, she produced a series of batik sarongs that combined colors and designs typical of two major batik centers of Java—a warm brown and *mengkudu* red from the Pesisir area. The *badan* on this sarong has been decorated with a *dlorong* design composed of alternating diagonal bands filled with a hook-like motif on a cream ground, typical of the Priangan area of West Java where it is known as *rereng*, and rows of ornate leaves on an indigo ground. The *kepala* has been decorated with a bouquet of carnations.

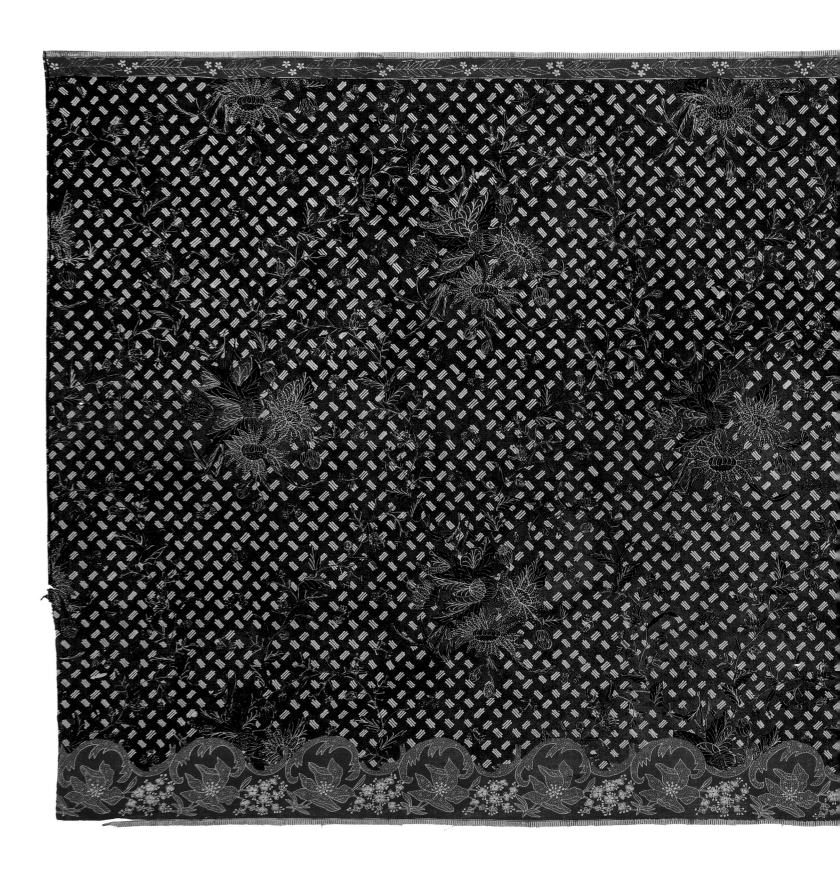

28

9　Sarong, signed "L Metz Pek", made by Mrs Lien Metzelaar (ca. 1855–1930), Pekalongan, ca. 1910.

While the *kepala* of this sarong features a large bouquet of bleeding hearts, the *badan* has been decorated with bunches of peonies on a background covered with a woven or plaited design. As Mrs Metzelaar used to work with an Arab dealer from Batavia (Jakarta), it is possible that the frequent appearance of woven patterns on her batik reflects the aesthetic preference of Arab Peranakan.

10 Kain buketan, signed "E v Zuylen", made in Mrs Eliza van Zuylen's workshop (1863–1947), Pekalongan, ca. 1930. Because of her lengthy career as a batik entrepreneur, Mrs van Zuylen's life and work are well documented. All the batik in the van Zuylen compound was decorated by hand (*batik tulis*) to the highest standards and was distinguished by its large floral bouquets cleanly delineated against solid backgrounds, often in pastel hues, accentuated by simple diagonal lines on the badan. Her floral inspiration was believed to come from Dutch horticulture books. Prior to World War II, *kain panjang* (long cloths) became popular among some Peranakan. Here, the classic van Zuylen *buketan* motif of gerbera flowers decorates this new type of wrapped skirt cloth. The dark colors indicate that this cloth was suitable for an older woman.

11 Sarong, signed "E v Zuylen", made in Mrs Eliza van Zuylen's workshop (1863–1947), Pekalongan, ca. 1930s. Motifs of large wading birds and water plants became popular on the north coast of Java in the 1920s and 1930s (see photo page 63). The drawing on the *badan* of this sarong was executed in a highly simplified way without the usual attention to detail characteristic of van Zuylen batik. It is possible, therefore, that the batik is a forgery that imitates the work of van Zuylen.

12 Sarong buketan, signed "E v Zuylen", made in Eliza van Zuylen's (1863–1947) workshop, Pekalongan, ca. 1920–1930. This batik is an Indo-European (Indische) interpretation of lotuses, which frequently decorate Lasem batik made in Chinese workshops. While the flowers are usually presented on an undyed cream background in Lasem, here the background is a deep red. The use of lotus flowers indicates that the sarong was meant for a Chinese Peranakan woman.

13 Sarong buketan, signed "E v Zuylen", made in Eliza van Zuylen's (1863–1947) workshop, Pekalongan, ca. 1900.
The dark, subdued colors of this sarong and its restrained decoration, with the *kepala* filled with abstract, geometric motifs and the *badan* bearing four elegant bouquets against a background grid of simple dots, would have appealed to affluent Muslim women from Sumatra. Eliza van Zuylen used to have clients also in that part of Indonesia and it was there that this sarong was purchased.

**14 Sarong buketan, signed "M. Coenraad. Patjitan",
Pacitan, 1890–1900.**
The Coenraad sisters opened a batik workshop in Pacitan
in southwestern East Java around 1880. The characteristic
feature of their work is a combination of Central Javanese
colors (indigo blue and soga brown) with floral motifs of
the Pesisir area. The large bouquets of chrysanthemums
that decorate the *badan* of this sarong indicate that it was
made for a Chinese customer.

40

15 Sarong buketan, signed "E Coenraad. Patjitan", Pacitan, ca. 1900–1910.
Unusually for the Coenraad sisters, this batik was executed in the Pesisir colors of indigo blue and *mengkudu* red. The exaggerated lines of the stems of the poppies on the *badan* point to the influence of the Art Nouveau style. Also remarkable is the extremely fine net-like decoration on the background. The *kepala* features another large floral arrangement of orchids and poppies surrounded by butter-flies, bees, small birds and a horseshoe. It is possible that this sarong was commissioned as part of a bridal trousseau.

16 Sarong buketan, signed "The Tie Siet Pekalongan", made in the The Tie Siet workshop, 1920–1930s.
The Tie Siet's batik workshop in Pekalongan was recognized as one of the best in the Pesisir area, and one that clearly showed The Tie Siet's Chinese heritage. This sarong illustrates the use of two non-traditional colors—orange and aqua—and simpler bouquets on a plain background. Four carefully executed bouquets of daffodils decorate the *badan* and *kepala*. Smaller renditions of the same flower run along the top and bottom of the sarong and also separate the *badan* from the *kepala*.

17 Sarong buketan kelengan, signed "The Tie Siet Pek", made in the The Tie Siet workshop, Pekalongan, 1930s.
Kain kelengan, blue and white batik cloths, were worn by Sino-Indonesian residents of the Pesisir during times of mourning. While the *kepala* and *badan* of this sarong have been decorated with four large bouquets of peonies, the most remarkable feature is the very elaborate grid-like background pattern which this workshop was famous for in the 1930s.

18 Sarong dlorong buketan, synthetic dyes, signed "The Tie Siet Pekalongan", made in the The Tie Siet workshop, Pekalongan, 1920–1930s.
Peonies are much loved by the Chinese for their bold size and colors. They are also associated with female beauty. Here, peonies dominate the diagonal bands (*dlorong*) on the *badan* as well as the large bouquet on the *kepala*.

**19 Sarong dlorong, synthetic dyes, signed "Kwee Nettie",
made in the Oey Soe Tjoen workshop, Kedungwuni, near
Pekalongan, 1930s.**
In 1925, Kwee Nettie (1905–98; Chinese name Kwee Tjoen
Giok), who came from a batik-making family in Batang,
married the great master of Sino-Javanese batik, Oey Soe

Tjoen. In the early years of their marriage, she signed her pieces with her European name, Kwee Nettie, but later used her husband's name. She also managed their joint workshop. This nine-color sarong is testimony to her love of color as well as her mastery in handling synthetic dyes. The type of decoration, made of wide vertical and diagonal bands, is known as *dlorong*. In the *badan*, the vertical bands of leaves and lotus flowers alternate with bands of jasmine blossoms and forget-me-nots. The *kepala* features the floral bands in a diagonal arrangement, a common feature of Pesisir batik of the 1920s and 1930s.

**20 Sarong buketan, signed "Oey Soe Tjoen Kedoengwoeni",
made in the Oey Soe Tjoen workshop, Kedungwuni, near
Pekalongan, 1930s.**

The workshop of Oey Soe Tjoen (1901–76) was famous for
creating the finest batik in Java. Oey Soe Tjoen was known
for his superb craftsmanship and attention to detail. The
care with which the motifs, primarily flowers and leaves in
bouquets, were drawn and shaded, such as the carnations
on this sarong, produced a unique three-dimensional effect
on his batik. Although such bouquets of flowers used to be
a popular feature of Pekalongan batiks made in the Indo-
European workshops, in the 1920s this style also became
popular on Chinese batik from the north coast of Java.

21 Sarong, signed "Oey Soe Tjoen. Kedoengwoeni", made in the Oey Soe Tjoen workshop, Kedungwuni, near Pekalongan, 1930s.
Cranes, Chinese symbol of immortality, are abundant on this sarong. While pairs of cranes feed among oversized plants and water lilies, other cranes fly overhead. The style of drawing and the colors of the motifs bear a resemblance to the gold-thread couched embroidery that is frequently found on Chinese ceremonial garments.

22 **Sarong dlorong buketan, signed "Nja Lie Boen In Koedoes", made by Njonja Lie Boen In, Kudus, 1920s.**
Lie Boen In was born in Pekalongan, but in later years moved to Kudus. However, the iconography of her batik indicates the strong influence of Pekalongan textiles. Her batik production was rather limited and her clients were

mainly members of her extended family. The *badan* on this sarong features three large floral bouquets composed of colorful poppies and blue and white forget-me-nots, while the diagonal bands (*dlorong*) on the *kepala* have been filled with birds and lily stems. The most striking feature of the sarong is its background, which is covered with extremely fine, densely worked diagonal lines, known as the *galaran* pattern.

Pages 50–63 Studio portraits of Chinese Peranakan women (except page 61) wearing fine north coast batik sarongs with lacy *kebaya* blouses.

23 Kain, Chinese workshop, north coast (Semarang or Lasem), second half 19th century. Chinese wedding procession (Arak-arakan Pengantin Cina).
Towards the end of the 19th century, batik was often made in the Pesisir area to commemorate special events. In the case of Chinese weddings, the fabrics were used as wedding gifts, presented by the family of the groom to the bride. At the top and bottom of this cloth, a joyful procession accompanies the young couple as the bride is taken from her family house to the house of the groom. Men are shown holding flags, banners and lanterns, and there are scores of musicians. The actual wedding ceremony is

presented in the center of the cloth, inside a series of pavilions. From left to right, in their respective family houses, the bride and groom undergo a series of rituals and are dressed in elaborate wedding costumes. The next pavilion features the newlyweds, sitting opposite each other at a table, marking their union by eating a ritual dish.

In the following scene, they pray at the ancestral pavilion. In the last building, probably the final stage of the wedding, the newlyweds serve tea to the family elders. The people standing behind the bride and groom are the ritual minders whose duty it is to make sure that all elements of this important ceremony are conducted in the correct way.

24 Sarong, Pekalongan, late 19th–early 20th century.
Batik sarongs made by Indo-European workshops for the colonial market in Java included depictions of famous fairytales, such as this one showing the story of Cinderella. The bottom half of the *badan* features, from right to left,

the two ugly sisters, the stepmother and Cinderella. In the upper half is a clock, the prince holding Cinderella's shoe and the heroine, running away with one foot bare. The *kepala* presents the happy ending, where the prince and

Cinderella are united under an oversized floral arrangement. The background has been densely covered with intricate filler motifs (*tanahan*). The sarong would probably have been made for a young Indo-European woman.

25 Kain, probably made in an Arab workshop in Pekalongan, early 20th century.

The minarets that frame the two arch-like structures, probably mosques, as well as the fact that the faces of all human beings have been disguised with bird-like features, suggest that this cloth was made in one of the Arab workshops in the Pesisir area. In the late 1920s, there were 130 batik workshops on Java run by members of the Arab Peranakan community. Different modes of transport, from hand-drawn to motor-propelled, are also depicted.

26 Sarong, probably made in an Arab workshop in Pekalongan, early 20th century.

The faces of all the living beings—humans, birds, dogs and even a horse—depicted in this rural scene have been dis-guised in some way. Some have been turned into floral-like forms. This feature, as well as the large bouquet of flowers, suggests that the cloth was produced in Pekalongan, in one of the many batik workshops run by Indonesian Arabs.

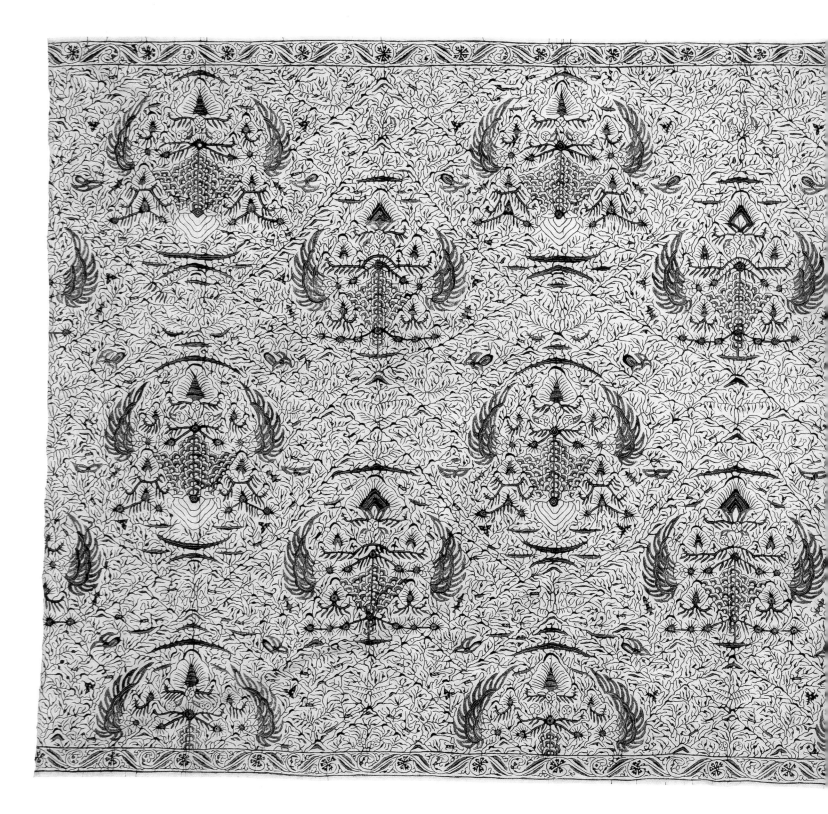

27 Sarong, made in the Masina family workshop, Trusmi, near Cirebon, late 19th century.
Whereas in Central Java a sarong is considered to be an everyday garment for commoners, in West Java it is also worn by the nobility. The motifs on this sarong indicate that it was made for a member of the Kesepuhan or Kanoman Sultanates of Cirebon. The *badan* features the *penganten* design, the wings of the mythical bird Garuda, known as *sawat* in Central Java, which was traditionally reserved for use by the Javanese nobility. Other important symbols are the tree of life, snakes (probably the serpent Naga) and mountains (Mount Meru, the abode of Hindu gods). The

main motifs are connected by a network of small sprouting plants and tendrils, in Central Java known as *semen* ("to grow", "to sprout"), which support life forces and assure prosperity. The *kepala* features an intricate patchwork-like *tumpal* design composed of different sized triangles (see also pages 80–1, 84–5). The batik decoration is of the *latar* *putih* (white background) type, whereby a layer of wax was applied to the background prior to the dyeing process, leaving only the outlines of the motifs uncovered. Technically, it is a very complex and time-consuming way of wax drawing that requires high manual dexterity and experience.

28 Sarong, Pesisir area, early 20th century.
The rooster, the most popular bird of Java, is the hero of
this batik, which may have been made for a devotee of
cock-fighting. The *badan* is filled with thousands of tiny

dots (*cocohan*) (see also pages 78–9). This effect has been
achieved by pricking the layer of wax with a set of fine
needles, and is typical of batik made in Lasem, Indramayu
and, occasionally, Cirebon.

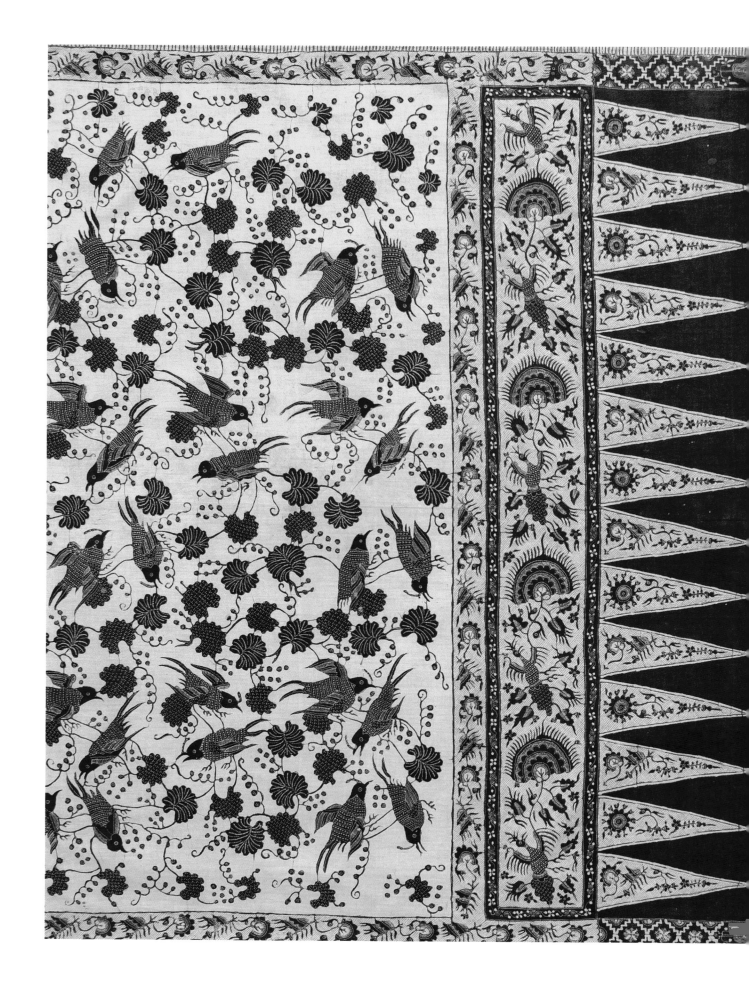

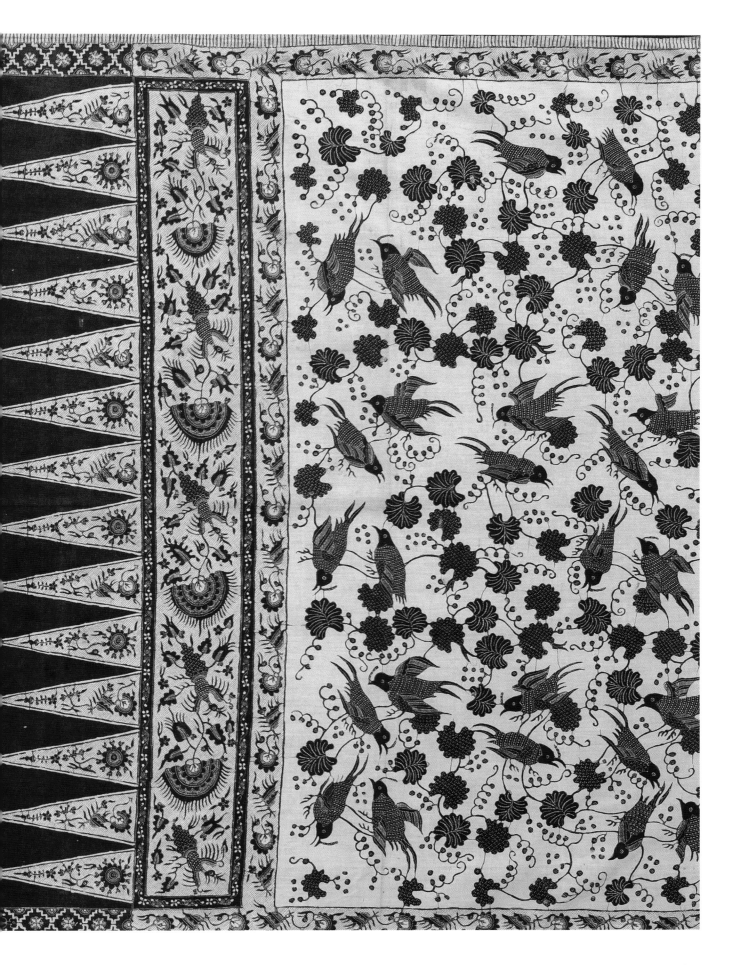

29 Sarong, probably Lasem, ca. 1890.
Swallows appear quite frequently on Pesisir batik, usually presented as a schematic bird figure. However, the decoration on this cloth is quite exceptional as it presents the birds in a multitude of positions—in various stages of flight and resting among curved plant stems. The brownish-red color is known as *ungon* and results from the over-dyeing of indigo and *mengkudu* red.

30 Sarong, probably Cirebon, ca. 1860–1880.
This is probably another batik associated with one of the Cirebon royal courts (*kraton*) (see pages 72–3). While it maintains the classic sarong composition, its *badan* has been decorated with motifs usually associated with the courts of Central Java, such as *lar*, the wing of the mythical bird Garuda. A dense and elaborate network of plant tendrils covers the background of the whole cloth. The execution of this sarong required great manual skill as the wax had to cover all areas except the outlines of the motifs.

31 Sarong, made in a Chinese workshop, probably Lasem, 1870–1880.
The *badan* of sarongs made in the 1880s in Lasem were often decorated with repetitive geometric designs, usually in the form of stars, crosses, rosettes, lozenges or polygons. On this sarong, the *tumpal* and *pinggir* feature carnations while the two *papan* have been filled with dragons, a mythical serpent (Naga) and probably a centipede, the latter symbolizing protection. The background of the whole cloth has been decorated with thousands of tiny dots (*cocohan*) (see pages 74–5).

32 Sarong, made in a Chinese workshop, Pesisir area, 1900–1910.
This sarong features a typical Pesisir motif, *ganggeng* or floating seaweed, yet included among the animals within it are mythical Chinese creatures, such as dragons with four claws and dragon-headed fish.

33 Sarong, Pesisir area, ca. 1880.
The *badan* of this cloth has been decorated with a *lung-lungan* design of fantastic birds and exuberant flowers, a typical Javanese rendition of Indian chintz. Dark colors indicate that the cloth was made for an older person. The thousands of tiny dots (*cocohan*) present in the *tumpal*, *papan* and *pinggir* sections indicate that the cloth was made in one of the workshops of Lasem, Cirebon or Indramayu.

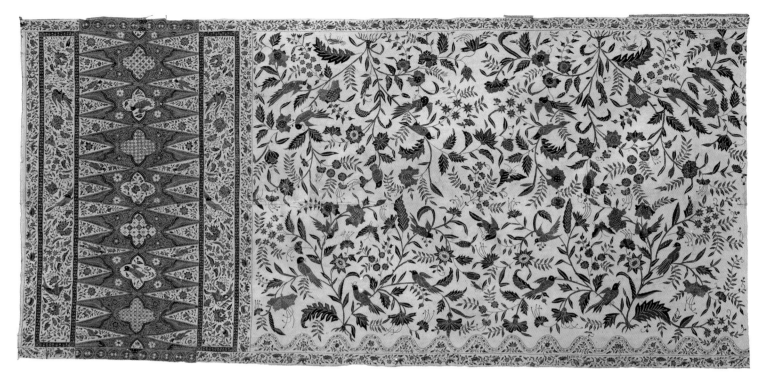

34 Sarong, made in a Chinese workshop, Pesisir area, ca. 1900.
The most remarkable feature of this sarong is its *kepala*, which is filled with *tumpal* motifs of alternating size, with a row of scalloped medallions runnng down the center. The *badan* features the tree of life motif and a multitude of small birds, butterflies and insects. The restrained colors of this sarong result from the use of indigo and brown dyes.

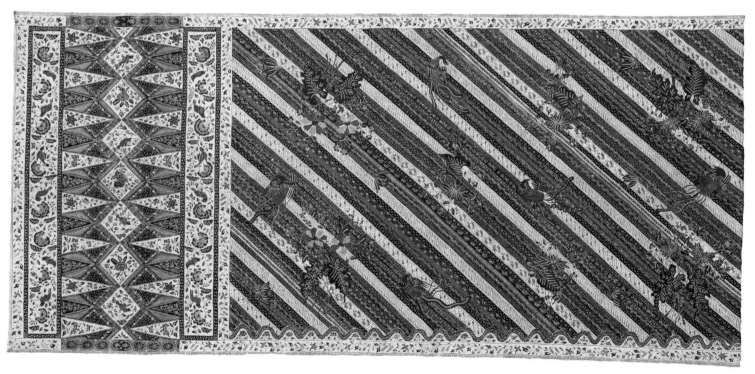

35 Sarong, made in a Chinese workshop, Pesisir area, second half 19th century.
This sarong harmoniously combines designs of Central Java and the Pesisir area. The *badan* features fine diagonal designs from the Yogyakarta and Surakarta batik tradition, over which are superimposed Pesisir motifs, such as bouquets of flowers, phoenixes and butterflies. The *kepala* has been decorated with a very complex design typical of batik produced in Chinese Peranakan workshops.

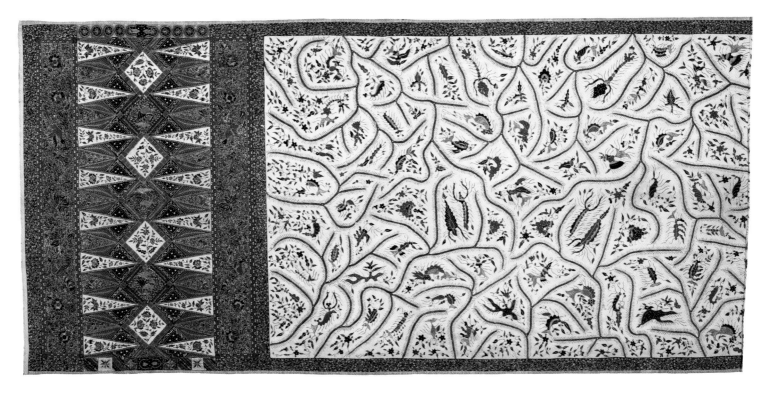

36　Sarong, made in a Chinese workshop, Pesisir area,
　　1900–1910.
A combination of floating seaweed and sea creatures on a
light background is one of the oldest motifs of the Pesisir area.

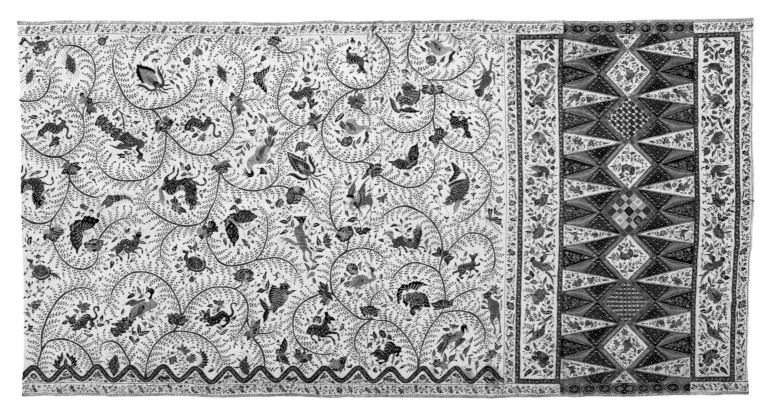

37　Sarong, made in a Chinese workshop, Pesisir area,
　　19th–20th century.
The *badan* of this sarong has been decorated with a version
of the zoo design, known on the north coast of Java as
drintin (from the Dutch *dieren tuin*). The animals have been
placed among the foating seaweed pattern, known as
ganggeng, popular in the Pesisir area. The decoration on the
kepala, with its triple diamond design, is quite remarkable
(see also pages 72–3, 84–5 and this spread).

38 Sarong, Lasem or Semarang, second half 19th century. Finely drawn egrets among ornate flowering trees point to an Indian chintz textile as the source of inspiration for this batik. Remarkably, each egret has been presented in a different position. While the *kepala* features the classic *tumpal* arrangement, the *papan* have been decorated with dense, intricate motifs of small birds and plants that echo the decoration of the main body of the sarong. An elaborate bow border (*booh*) frames both the *papan* and runs along the lower edge (*pinggir*) of the cloth.

39 Sarong, probably Lasem, late 19th–early 20th century.
Lasem batik was once famous for its floral motifs and beautifully drawn Chinese motifs in deep red and blue on a light ground. The elaborate plants shown on the *badan* of this sarong, with their large blossoms and roots, were undoubtedly inspired by the tree of life motif frequently found on chintz trade cloths from the Coromandel coast of India (see also no. 34, page 80 and pages 86–7). The complex arrangement of the *kepala* (see also pages 80–1) and a very fine bow border (*booh*) running along the lower edge of the cloth made this sarong an exquisite festive garment.

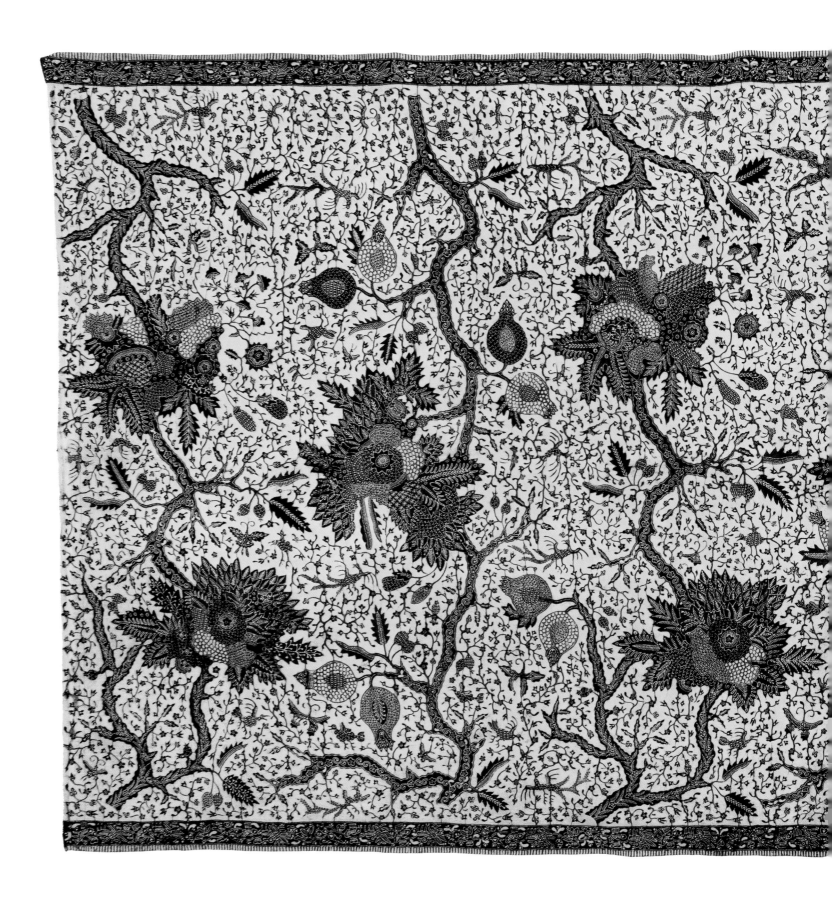

40 Sarong, made in an Indo-European workshop, Pesisir area, 1870–1880.
The decoration on this cloth makes a reference to the tree of life motif (see also no. 34 page 80 and pages 85–6). It was commonly found on imported chintz textiles from India's Coromandel coast, which were much favored by Indo-European women in the East Indies. It is not surprising that numerous batik cloths produced in the 19th century in Chinese as well as Indo-European workshops along the north coast of Java replicated chintz designs in the batik technique.

41 Kain, made in a Chinese workshop, probably Lasem, 1920s.
The wide diagonal bands decorating the main section of this wrapped around skirt have been filled alternately with bouquets of flowers and old favorites of the Pesisir area—marine and aquatic creatures, such as goldfish, prawns, crabs and snails, floating among seaweed (*ganggeng*). The

half *kepala* on each end of the *badan* is of two different background colors, one red, the other black, and different designs. By reversing the folding, the wearer was able to make use of two different designs from a single piece of cloth. The darker design was usually reserved for daytime use and the lighter design for evening.

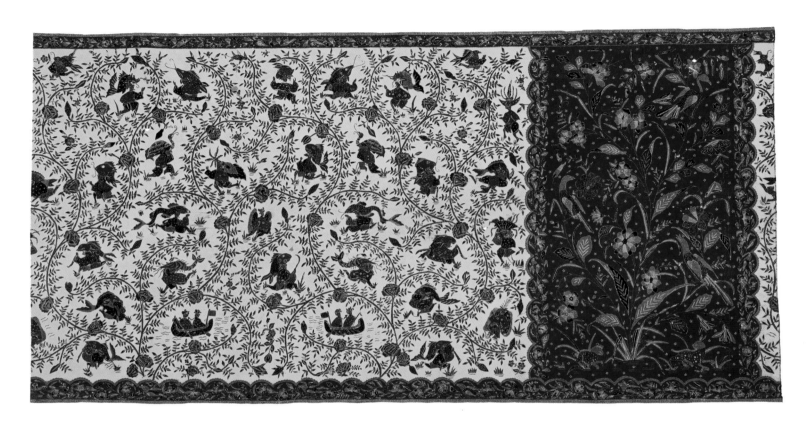

42 Sarong, made in a Chinese workshop, Pesisir area.
This cloth is a Chinese rendition of floral sarongs created in the Indo-European workshops of Pekalongan, such as the one run by Eliza van Zuylen. The *badan* illustrates a Chinese folk story of two greedy and cruel officials who have been turned into giant fish. The floral vines enclosing the motifs are a typical feature of north coast batik compositions. The *kepala* features a classic bouquet of flowers in the Pekalongan style as well as two rabbits, a symbol of fertility and abundance in Chinese culture.

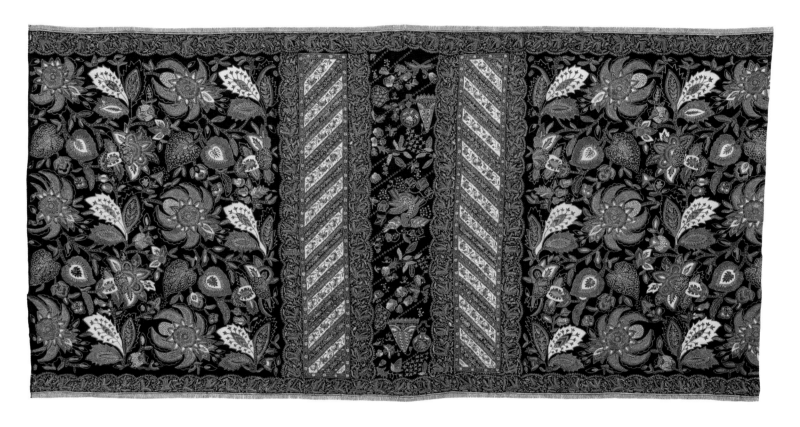

43 Sarong, made in an Indo-European workshop, Pesisir area, ca. 1860.

The dramatic oversized blossoms on the *badan* of this sarong have their origins in the style of 17th–18th century Indian chintz cloth that was traded to Indonesia. Most unusual is the *kepala* of this sarong, which has a narrow centerfield dominated by extraordinarily wide *papan* borders filled with diagonal bands. Another prominent feature is the wide and elaborate *booh* (bow border), a scalloped band, that encloses both sides of each *papan* and runs along the top and bottom of the cloth.

44 Kain pagi–sore, north coast or Madura Island, ca. 1890–1900.

This *kain*, an example of what is known in Java as *kain pagi–sore* or "morning–afternoon cloth", illustrates the concept of two skirts in one or reversible clothing. By reversing the folding, the wearer is able to make use of two different designs on the same cloth for different occasions and times and to strikingly different effect. The darker design was usually preferred for daywear and the lighter one for evening. Although the two "halves" of most *pagi–sore*

sarongs are divided diagonally, unusually this piece is divided vertically. Each half has a *badan* and a *kepala* in totally contrasting designs, drawing styles and colors. While on the lighter half the long-necked birds and other creatures are recognizable, on the darker half the figures of egrets and lions have distorted features, similar to the way in which motifs on batik made in Arab workshops along the north coast were disguised or stylized. At times, a similar approach towards camouflaging animal figures was adopted in batik made on Madura Island.

45 **Sarong, made in an Indo-European workshop,
    Pesisir area, late 19th century.**
    The striking feature of this sarong is its extra wide *kepala*,
    which contains pairs of courting birds as the central motif.

The *badan* has been decorated with simplified butterflies,
grapes, seed pods, floral sprigs and probably balloons or
hand fans.

46 Sarong buketan, probably Pekalongan, late 19th–early 20th century.
This sarong has not been signed, yet the quality of its wax drawing equals the best examples of batik made in the workshops of Metzelaar, Jans or van Zuylen. Its decoration features a multitude of delicately drawn flowers—fuchsias, pansies, cornflowers and gerberas. A closely worked floral garland runs down both sides of the *papan* enclosing the *kepala* and along the lower edge of the cloth. Butterflies, small birds and a couple of horseshoes contribute to the festive feel of the sarong, which might have been part of a bridal trousseau for an Indo-European woman.

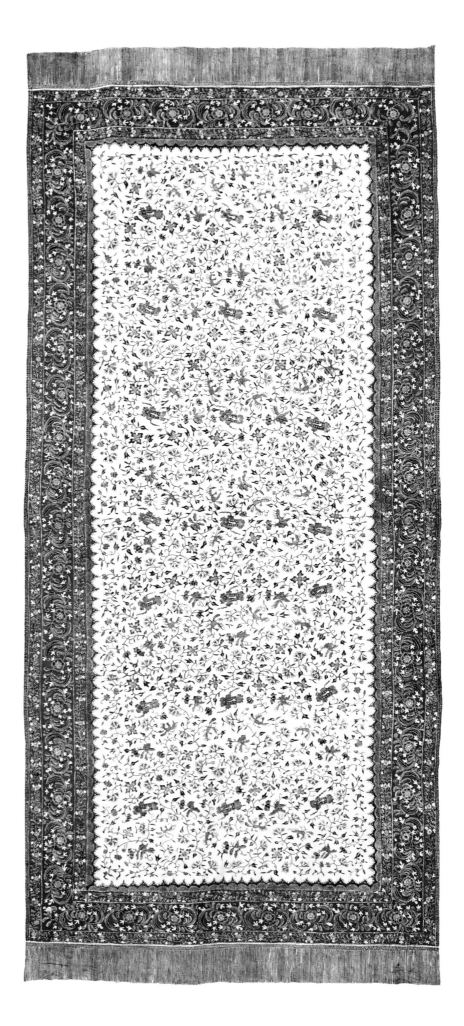

47
Kudhung jufri (head and shoulder cloth), made in Cirebon or Lasem for the Sumatran market, early 20th century.

The name of this large shawl with its characteristic lightly colored central field originates from the Arab Al Juffri family, famous entrepreneurs in Jambi. The cloth was made in a Peranakan workshop in the Pesisir area, probably in Cirebon or Lasem. The main field contains popular but subdued Chinese motifs, such as carnations and phoenixes. The ends of the cloth have been decorated with rows of *kemada* (imitation fringe), a feature that further exemplifies the similarity of this batik cloth to floral carpets from Persia.

48
Kudhung kra mutung (head and shoulder cloth), made in Jambi, late 19th–early 20th century.
The centerfield of this shawl has been decorated with *merak merem* or *merak ngeram* (broody peacock), a design that traces its origins to the Middle Eastern palmetto figure. The deep red floral border surrounding the main field also shows certain similarities to Middle Eastern textile decoration. Dark *mengkudu* red and dark indigo blue were favored by the people of Jambi. In addition to batik made on the north coast of Java for the Sumatran market in the 19th century, local batik production developed in Jambi. It is highly probable that this cloth was made there.

49

Kain basurek, made in Cirebon or Batavia (Jakarta) for the Sumatran market, 19th–20th century.

Kain basurek (from *kain bersurat*, "written cloth") is a fabric decorated with Arabic inscriptions or imitations of these. Arab tradition has long discouraged the representation of living things in Muslim art and decoration. This has impacted the designs and motifs on batik and its use. This cloth illustrates a patchwork of stylized floral designs and inserts containing highly simplified Arabic inscriptions. The light-colored fields at top right and bottom left contain a reversed image of the word Allah. The inscriptions in the central rhomboids probably indicate the two most frequent appellations of Allah— Ar-Rahman and Ar-Rahim (Kind and Merciful). Although the cloth is supposed to have religious significance, the inscriptions have, in fact, been given the same significance as other motifs.

50

Kain basurek, made in Cirebon or Batavia (Jakarta) for the Sumatran market, 19th–20th century.
On this cloth, the borders of the three central rhomboids contain highly simplified inscriptions of the names of Allah and Muhammad. This could be an expression of *shahada*, the Muslim profession of faith that encompasses these two names ("There is no God but Allah and Muhammad is His Messenger"). In the floral background, which is reminiscent of Persian carpets, there are several *tughra*, the calligraphic monogram or emblematic signature of Ottoman rulers. It is likely that the inscriptions were made by a person who was not well-versed in writing Arabic script.

51
Kain basurek, made in Cirebon or Batavia (Jakarta) for the Sumatran market, 19th–20th century.
The surface of this cloth has been divided into a number of geometric fields, squares and rectangles, some of which are filled with arabesque motifs that imitate Arabic characters. Only in the square fields, placed inside large rhomboid figures, is it possible to recognize very simplified inscriptions of Allah and Muhammad. The person who made this batik was not particularly skilled at writing Arabic script. In parts of Sumatra, it is believed that cloths with Arabic inscriptions have protective or talismanic powers.

52
**Ceremonial hanging, made in a
Chinese workshop, probably Lasem,
late 19th century.**
While the major feature of this cloth
is a pair of phoenixes enclosed in a
centrally placed roundel, the other
elements—oversized flowers,
decorative tree trunks and ornate
leaves—echo the tree of life motifs
that frequently used to decorate 19th-
century sarongs made on the north
coast of Java (see no. 34 page 80 and
pages 85–6, 86–7 and 92–3). A row of
swastikas or *banji*, emblem of good
fortune, forms a simple grid-like frame
around the bold floral patterns that
cover most of the hanging (see also
pages 106, 111 and 122–3).

53 Sprei (bed cover), made in a Chinese workshop, probably Lasem, 19th–20th century.
A favorite motif on much of Lasem batik comprises fantastical birds floating among flowering branches. For this reason, fabrics decorated in this way are known as *kain laseman*. Here, a multitude of large phoenixes flying among branches covered with blossoms and seeds of various flowers has lifted a rather common composition into one with more dramatic overtones. The well-defined swastika or *banji* motif bordering the two rectangular fields carries a secular symbolism of good fortune on this textile.

54 Sprei (bed cover), made in a Chinese workshop, probably Lasem, 19th–20th century.
The multitude of motifs symbolizing good luck on this cloth—phoenixes, lions, dragons, bats, roosters, deer and pots of various flowers—suggest that it was created to ensure prosperity to a newlywed couple from a Chinese Peranakan family in Java.

55
Ceremonial hanging, 105 x 205 (+30) cm, made in a Chinese workshop, Pesisir area, 19th–20th century.
This highly elaborate cloth featuring lotus plants, phoenixes, roosters, hens and even a couple of acrobats dancing on an elephant, was probably used as a hanging for a nuptial bed in a Chinese Peranakan home. The symbols stand for happiness and long life and also indicate a wish for many sons (the flowering lotus plant). Unusually for such fabrics, the layer of wax has been deliberately cracked, resulting in an irregular red veining on the background.

56 Door hanging, 2 x 77 x 232 (+32) cm, made in a Chinese workshop, Pesisir area.
This festive door hanging was probably used during Chinese New Year celebrations. The multitude of creatures decorating the cloth represent three realms—water (fish, prawns, crabs and turtles), land (deer, stags and chickens) and air (birds and butterflies). According to Chinese beliefs, each of these creatures adds a symbolic message or sentiment to the textile, for example, fish symbolize plentitude and abundance, turtles a long life and butterflies summer, beauty and romance.

57 Celana (trousers), 125 x 106 cm, Pesisir area, probably Pacitan.

In the 19th century, trousers (*celana*) became the informal dress of Javanese (see photo left of knife sharpeners, ca. 1890) as well as European and Chinese residents of Java, as they suited the tropical climate much better than tight European garments. This pair is decorated with bold Chinese-inspired motifs on a cream background—birds and butterflies among foliage and, on the ground, facing tigers, one of the most revered animals in Chinese culture, representing power and courage. The bottom of each leg has a band composed of meandering flowers sandwiched between rows of swastika (*banji*).

58 Batik portrait, signed "Be Jan Khing Banjoemas 26 Juni 1931", 63 x 117 cm, Banyumas, Central Java, 1931.
Portraits are a relatively rare genre of Javanese batik. This one was probably commissioned to celebrate a milestone in the life of a Chinese lady, possibly a significant birthday, who was a resident of the Banyumas regency in the 1930s.

The portrait indicates that she was a modern, emancipated woman, interested in fashion.

Pages 113–21, 129, 132–41 Studio portraits of Javanese from all walks of life wearing batik made in Central Java with traditional motifs, such as the *parang* and *kawung*.

Goede mid
dag yyffrouw
5-8-'26

59 **Kain panjang, made in the Pesisir area for the Sumatran market, 1920–1930.**
This batik cloth is decorated with a small selection of figures from the Javanese shadow play (*wayang kulit*), which traditionally performs narratives derived from the Hindu epics, the *Ramayana* and *Mahabharata*. As the Sumatran audience was not as knowledgeable as the Javanese about *wayang*, each figure has been signed with the name of the hero it represents. The background of the cloth is covered with the Chinese *banji* or swastika motif, most often used as a border motif (see pages 105, 106 and 111).

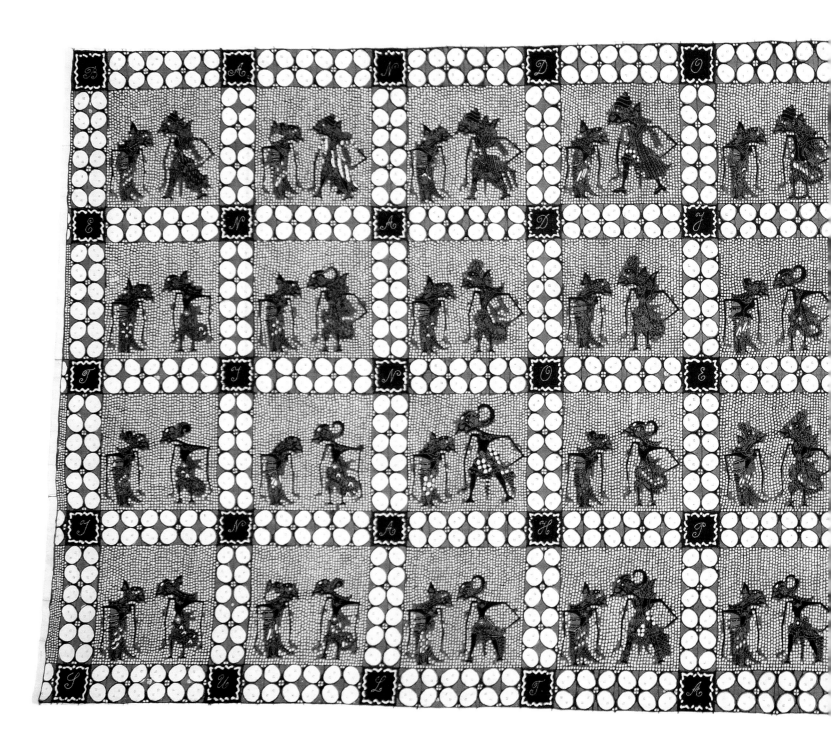

60 Kain panjang, Yogyakarta, 1930s.
This composition, featuring multiple pairs of figures from
the *wayang* shadow theater, is known as *ciptoning*. The
bands that separate the figures are filled with a variation
of the *kawung* or circular pattern that at one time could
be worn only by members of the sultans' families and high

officials in Central Java. Although the *kawung* motif usually consists of parallel rows of ellipses in an over-all design, here groups of ovals are arranged to form white, four-petaled flowers (see photos pages 114, 116, 117, 119, 121, 133, 135 and 137 of Javanese men and women wearing sarongs with variations of the *kawung* motif). The background of the cloth is covered with the *dele kecer* (scattered soy bean) motif, at times also interpreted as grains of rice, which stands for abundance and prosperity (see photos pages 115, 121 and 132). Batik sarongs featuring *wayang* figures were considered suitable for older, experienced and highly respected people.

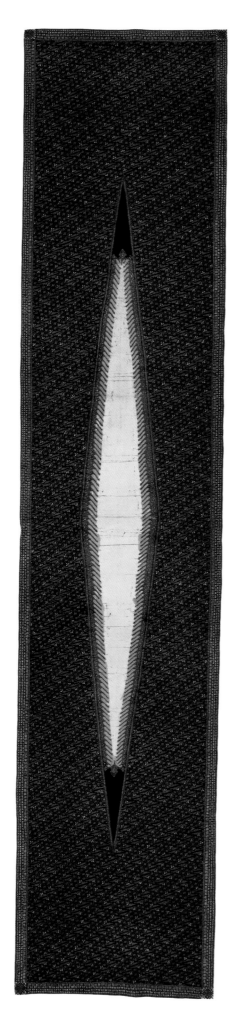

61
Kemben (breast cloth), batik,
Central Java.
Up until the 20th century, a *kemben*
or breast cloth was a part of official
female dress at the Central Javanese
courts and is still occasionally worn by
court dancers. It comprises a narrow
strip of cloth about 250 cm long and
75 cm wide, which is wound tightly
around the chest, leaving the shouders
bare (see photo page 138). The cloth
may be decorated in a single technique,
such as batik, or combined with
stitch-dyeing (*tritik*) or other techniques.
The central diamond-shaped figure
(*sindangan*) used to be lined with very
fine pink silk cloth, the remains of which
are still visible in the *cemukiran* ('flame')
section that surrounds the central
undyed field. The remaining part of the
cloth has been covered with a diagonal
batik design from the *parang* group.
Today, the *kemben* has been largely
replaced by the *kebaya*, a long-sleeved
tailored blouse usually decorated with
lace and embroidery (see photos pages
114–121, 132–41 of Javanese women).

62
Kemben (breast cloth), batik,
Central Java.
The *sindangan* on this *kemben*
has been lined with blue silk cloth.
The corners of the *kemben* have been
marked with white, four-petal *kawung*
motifs (see page 125).

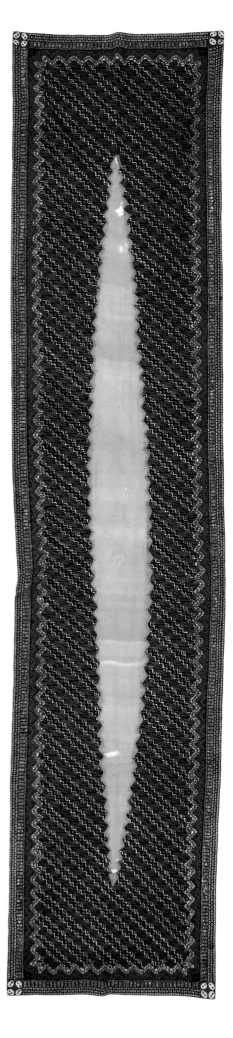

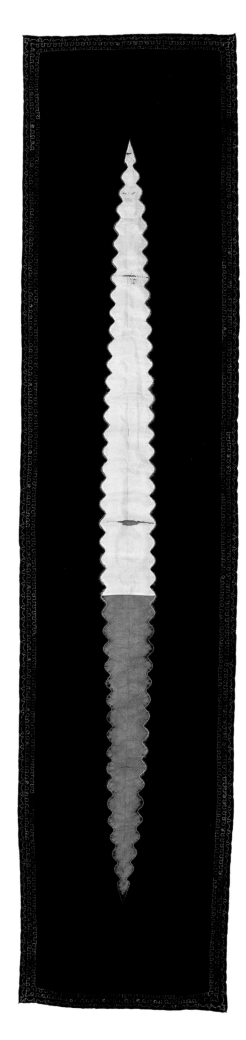

63
Kemben (breast cloth), tritik,
Central Java.
All the motifs on this cloth have been
created with the very fine technique of
stitch-dyeing (*tritik*). The *sindangan* has
been lined with red and white silk cloth.

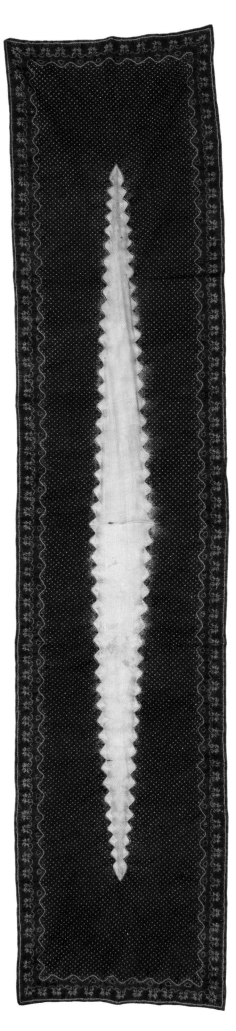

64
Kemben (breast cloth), tritik,
Central Java.
All the motifs of this cloth have
been created using the *tritik*
technique. The *sindangan*
has been lined with very fine,
light green silk cloth.

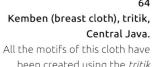

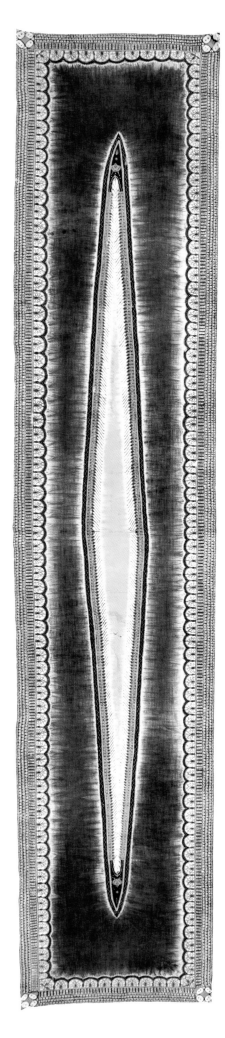

65
Kemben, batik and tritik, Central Java.
The cloth has been decorated with batik, applied as the first technique, and *tritik*, applied on completion of the batik process. While the batik technique was used to produce the brown bands running along the edges of the cloth and the flame-like *cemukiran* motif surrounding the *sindangan*, the *tritik* method was applied to two colors, the blue and light beige of the central field. The cloth was used by women of the Javanese aristocracy as a festive garment, wrapped around the torso (see page 138).

66
Kain kembangan, jumputan and batik, Central Java.
Multicolored *kemben* decorated with the *jumputan* technique are known as *kain kembangan* (cloth of flowers). In this method of resist-dyeing, small sections of the cloth were raised and strongly tied. On completion of the dyeing (here, in blue), top parts of the tied sections were uncovered and painted green, red and yellow. Batik was used to create the brown and dark blue bands that run along the edges of the cloth and surround the *sindangan*. As an additional decoration, the central field has been lined with an appliqué of fine yellow silk. Due to the cost of silk and the technical complexity, only half of the *kemben*, the one visible when worn, has been decorated.

67 Decorative hanging, 150 x 34 cm, probably made in the Masina family workshop, Trusmi, near Cirebon. In the late 19th century, some batik workshops on Java began production of decorative fabrics for European customers. Although the cloths frequently featured Javanese motifs, such as the shadow theater figures (*wayang*) on this cloth, the style of the decoration was adjusted to suit the taste of European customers. The bodies of the figures have been highlighted with gold leaf (or gold dust), a technique called *prada*.

I. ChiLau
4-8-25
Dk.

My Introduction to the World of Batik

Donald Harper

In the early 1970s, I was working in Amsterdam for a small scientific publishing company, a subsidiary of Elsevier Publishing, which published a wide variety of books and other materials in both Dutch and English. One day, a newly released book, *Three Faces of Indonesia: A Photographic Essay by Co Rentmeester*, landed on my desk. The jacket carried a stunning photograph of a lush, green rice paddy. The scene was so compelling that I eagerly opened the book to see what lay between the covers.

To cut a long story short, that was the day a whole new world opened before me and marked one of the most important turning points in my life. After examining the book, I decided then and there to make an extended journey to Indonesia and do whatever it would take to make that dream come true. The first priority was to save as much money as possible, so for the next year I stopped going to my favorite Amsterdam pubs and lived like a hermit.

Eventually, when I felt I had enough funds to last for at least a year, I resigned from Elsevier. My boss was surprised that I wanted to leave such a good, well-paying job and urged me to just take a leave of absence. But being young and adventurous, I had a feeling that better things lay ahead. I bid farewell to Holland and headed for Yogyakarta in Central Java via Thailand, Malaysia and Singapore.

On my journey south from Chiang Mai to Jakarta, a leisurely trip that lasted more than two months, I decided to visit a seaside village just outside of Kota Bharu on the east coast of Malaysia that had a famous beach called the Beach of Passionate Love, the name of which has since been diluted to the more culturally acceptable Moonlight Beach. It was there that I got my first whiff of molten beeswax permeating the air, which I soon discovered was the unmistakable smell of batik being produced somewhere in the vicinity. Wandering around the village, I saw hundreds of freshly made batik cloths drying on clothes lines in the wind. That was the day I discovered batik.

I don't recall exactly why I deliberately chose to start my Indonesian adventure in the Central Javanese city of Yogyakarta rather than the more seductive and trendy Bali, but I had read that "Yogya" was a highly regarded place in its own right and considered by many to be the cultural capital of Java. It was also one of the most important centers of traditional batik production in Indonesia.

At the time, Pasar Beringharjo, a market on Malioboro Street, was the *pusat* (center) for buying old batik and *kebaya*. *Kebaya* are the amazingly intricate lace blouses that were once worn by Peranakan (Chinese), Dutch and some indigenous women in the days of *tempo doeloe*, or the colonial era. Peter Lee of Singapore recently published a comprehensive book titled *Sarong Kebaya*, which artfully illustrates the beauty and history of these garments and how they were routinely worn throughout the Malay and Indonesian archipelagos in the 19th and early 20th centuries. Even a novice like me could instantly see that such old, intricately made textiles were special treasures, indeed exceptional works of art, and here they were being sold, incongruously, in a hot, grungy market full of otherwise mundane, everyday items normally found in a huge Asian market.

Although I figured I had enough money to last for about a year in Indonesia, the thought of running out of funds lingered at the back of my mind. Once I had got my first taste of freedom roaming around Southeast Asia, I determined never to return to the nine to five rat race again. I decided I had better invest my remaining funds in a small enterprise rather than let what little money I had left fritter away. Even though I don't come from a merchant background and really had no idea how to run a business, I made Pasar Beringharjo my "office" and went there every day. Slowly but surely, I learned about batik from the entrepreneurial *ibu* (women) who bought and sold old batik and *kebaya* for a living. While studying under those unlikely mentors, who themselves wore batik every day, I began to learn about the many subtleties of batik craftsmanship and what the masters looked for in a great piece. Before long, I could readily distinguish a *cap* (stamped) batik from a *tulis* (hand-drawn) one and also those that were made with natural as opposed to chemical dyes. Eventually, I was able to instinctively identify the exceptional pieces and whether they were in the Chinese, Dutch or Javanese styles. Selecting good *kebaya*, on the other hand, wasn't nearly as complicated as choosing batik but I did have to carefully examine them under the poor lighting conditions of the market to make sure there weren't any small holes or repairs.

One by one, I cautiously assembled a collection of pieces, leaving myself just enough money to pay for a one-way ticket and expenses to Biarritz and San Tropez in France, both popular summer holiday destinations for affluent Europeans. It was make or break time. I dreaded the thought that if nobody bought my wares, I might have to return to Holland and—perish the thought—have to ask for my old job back. On the other hand, if everything went according to plan, I'd be heading back to Indonesia at the end of the summer with my coffers replenished.

Fortunately, the gods looked favorably on me and things worked out well. The *kebaya*, in particular, were very popular in fashion-conscious San Tropez. I set up a little makeshift stand along the beautiful waterfront where all the magnificent multimillion dollar yachts were docked. I watched elegant couples returning arm in arm to their gleaming, brightly illuminated boats from the local bistros. Many of them would do a double-take when they saw the gorgeous textiles I had neatly folded on the sidewalk atop a humble blanket, and some would stop and ask me questions about them. Quite a few of the young women insisted on trying on the *kebaya* right there in the street! Although the batik fabrics were not quite as popular as the *kebaya*, it wasn't long before I only had a few left. Incidentally, many of those same textiles are today quite rare and expensive but back then I was happy to sell them for a modest price.

After that successful summer foray in the south of France, it seemed that my idea to focus on batik had been validated. I breathed a sigh of relief and flew back to Indonesia with a renewed determination to further my knowledge of the cloth.

Thus began my long relationship—some might call it obsession—with the world of vintage batik and subsequently other Indonesian antique textiles such as *songket* and *ikat*. As luck would have it, I met my dear friend Rudolf Smend in Yogyakarta early on in this endeavor. With his encouragement and support, we began a close collaboration that has lasted for some forty years. Rudolf was a pioneer batik collector and together we acquired what are arguably some of the best old batik fabrics ever made. Many of Rudolf's personal collection of top quality pieces have now been acquired by a number of museums and first-class collectors whose batik collections will probably end up in museums sooner or later. As for my own collection of old batik, it is now "housed" in my personal online museum called the East Indies Museum (www.eastindiesmuseum.com).

I could go on and on about the many adventures and wonderful people I have met as a result of being an aficionado of Indonesian textiles, including, as it turns out, my wife who is Vietnamese. In some mysterious and wonderful way, she came into my life through my interest in batik. Batik has thus been the continuing narrative that for the past forty years has taken me from Kota Bharu to Yogyakarta to San Tropez and, finally, to my current home in Saigon. I feel obliged to say a huge *terima kasih* to Indonesia. The country and its people have given me so much to be grateful for and I will always consider Indonesia my second home.

Batik and I
Jonathan Hope

My collection of Javanese batik spends most of the time safely housed in a cupboard, although much of it was recently displayed, juxtaposed with Indian trade cloths, in an exhibition called *Heirlooms* at the 2013 Edinburgh International Festival where it was seen by several thousand people. The show's popularity surprised me but should not have as a captive audience of art lovers could not fail to respond to the textiles' aesthetic beauty let alone the depth and other-worldliness of those from Central Java.

On occasion, I take three or four *kain* out of their hiding place and admire them with appreciative friends. There is a faint rustling sound as I unfold the cloths, which instantly transports me back to the gentle experience of traveling in Java at intervals over the past forty years and being shown countless cloths decorated in numerous styles through the infinitely painstaking process of *batik tulis*.

My first visit to Indonesia was a somewhat "hippy" affair in 1974–5. After a few months of absorbing this strange but unthreatening tropical environment that was so unlike home I began to notice the sarongs worn by the Balinese, especially when they embarked on their long processions to holy places. A few of the touristic shops in the Kuta area, mostly shacks along the edge of the beach, sold old textiles, and one day I spotted two or three delightful Pekalongan-style sarongs in pastel shades on the finest cotton imaginable. I learned that they were from the north coast of Java and presumably responded to their designs' European flavor. I discovered the more traditional and mysterious Central Javanese work a little later. These became my first Indonesian textiles and I had no idea that so much of the next four decades would be devoted to the medium, from Javanese batik to antique European embroidery via the traditional cloths of virtually the rest of the world. Nonetheless, batik remains my first textile love.

During the late 1970s, both American and European textile design was greatly influenced by north coast batik and many of my prettiest Pekalongan pieces found their way into the archive of a leading Paris fashion designer. I started to search for old textiles, usually weavings, in the antique shops of Holland and found a few excellent Indische batik sarongs there, including those bearing signatures, and became familiar with the work of J. Jans and E. van Zuylen. Some of my finds were acquired by the Victoria and Albert Museum and others now reside in Australia's National Gallery.

While traveling in Central Java, I became fascinated by the ancient traditions of the courts of Solo (formerly Surakarta) and Yogyakarta and learned how local syncretic spiritual beliefs could be deciphered from the soga brown, indigo and cream batik compositions, such as those bearing the ancient diagonally aligned *parang* ("knife") design and the circular *kawung* motif so prominent in many of the studio photos of Central Javanese reproduced on pages 113–21 and 132–41 of this book. I was fortunate to meet Go Tik Swan (K. R. T. Hardjonagoro), the legendary batik designer, former court dancer and aficionado of Javanese culture, who regaled me with descriptions of court ceremonies. He showed me how to look into the designs of traditional batik and find hidden statements of local spiritual and cosmological beliefs. When I see fine court batik today, I can almost hear *gamelan* music hanging in the air wherever I may be.

In 1990, there was a festival of Indonesia in and around London's Royal Festival Hall called *Island to Island*. It included Balinese ballet, Javanese *gamelan*, archival film footage from the Horniman Museum's library, *warung* (food stalls) and even *becak* (pedicab) rides along the riverbank. A gallery was constructed out of screens on the mezzanine level and this contained a selection of batik from my collection. In their reviews, the *Financial Times* and *The Spectator* both made the observation that fine batik is more than a craft; it is indeed a fine art.

I enjoy sharing my enthusiasm for these loveliest of world textiles whenever given the opportunity, and have written several articles on different aspects of the subject for *Hali* magazine, including a profile of Rudolf Smend. Occasionally, I am invited to give a lecture on batik, most recently at London's School of Oriental and African Studies (SOAS) at the University of London. When I do so, I am struck by the realization that I know only a little of the complex culture of traditional Java from which these glorious cloths emerge.

Right A youth wearing a mixture of European and Javanese garments.

Attracted by Javanese Culture
Annegret Haake

In 1970, I joined a guided tour to Southeast Asia, the first tour run by Garuda Indonesia Airlines. Over three weeks we traveled from Singapore to North Sumatra, West Java, Sulawesi, East Java, Bali and Central Java. We saw the houses and graves of the Batak and Toraja, the tea plantations of Java, climbed a volcano, visited the temples of Bali and the ancient Buddhist and Hindu monuments of East and Central Java. Yogyakarta was the last stage of that interesting but tiring trip. The only information I had previously known about Indonesia was that there were shadow puppets, batik and *nasi goreng* (fried rice). Then I met many friendly people everywhere; we communicated using "hands and feet". On the last day, three of us hired a taxi to find a souvenir for a friend and ended up at Batik Winotosastro.

After my return to Frankfurt, the manager of Garuda Airlines asked me for information about the trip, which led shortly after to the establishment of the Frankfurt German-Indonesian Association. Four hundred Indonesian nurses arrived in our area and needed our help to integrate. These new contacts led me to visit Yogya again in 1974, and I found Batik Winotosastro near the hotel where I stayed. Since my brief visit in 1970, the shop had changed a great deal, but it still offered the traditional Yogya designs.

When Pak Winotosastro saw my interest, he told his staff to "let her open all the cupboards". This I did, and every day I came back having made new friends. As Pak Winotosastro was one of the founders of Gabungan Koperasi Batik Indonesia (GKBI, Association of Indonesian Batik Co-operatives), he and his daughter Haryani joined a delegation to explore the opportunities for selling batik at the Frankfurt Trade Fair in 1976. Together with his daughters Sugiarti and Haryani, we arranged an exhibition at a bank, Frankfurter Sparkasse von 1822.

I have been involved with Javanese batik ever since, communicating with the Winotosastro family by phone, or whenever we meet, about methods, the chemistry of ingredients, and the meaning of motifs and their grouping. I had the opportunity to publish a book in 1984 which has now been translated into Indonesian. My job as a chemical technician at the Institute of Crystallography, University of Frankfurt, involved preparing materials for lectures. For symmetry exercises, I collected folk art designs and found the richest choice in traditional Javanese batiks—thirteen of the seventeen possible types. Haryani made a beautiful batik in a patchwork style that we introduced to the scientists at the conference of the European Crystallographic Meeting held in Marrakech in 2007.

Now that batik is on the UNESCO World Cultural Heritage list, we frequently introduce this wonderful art form together in publications and exhibitions.

About the Author

Since 1976, Annegret Haake has organized numerous exhibitions on Javanese batik, all of them accompanied by lectures and publications in relevant journals and books. After her retirement from the Institute of Crystallography at the University of Frankfurt/Main in 1993, she was appointed Honorary Lecturer of Javanese Batiks and Shadow Play at the Institute of Southeast Asian Studies. Exhibitions curated by her have been shown at private and official galleries as well as scientific congresses on crystallography, symmetry and textiles in Europe, America, Asia and Africa.

Annegret Haake's book *Javanische Batik* was published in 1984. It was followed, in 1993, by *Wayang Kulit*, a catalogue of her collection of shadow puppets. A booklet explaining the examples on display was published for each event.

In 2011, Annegret Haake participated in the World Batik Summit in Jakarta where she spoke on "Bringing Batik to the World Using Tambal and Composition". In 2012, she took part in an exhibition of Indonesian batik organized by EKONID (the German-Indonesian Chamber of Industry and Commerce) at the Galeri Nasional in Jakarta.

68 Kain panjang, signed "Oey Soe Tjoen Kedungwuni Java 104", near Pekalongan, 1980.

This *buketan* (bouquet) type of cloth has been created using an extremely fine batik technique in two shades of blue on a clear white background (*latar putih*). To achieve the clean white background, the family of Oey Soe Tjoen developed a method of preserving it during the waxing and coloring processes, which can last from several months to two years. The *buketan*-type sarong was inspired by herbaria (drawings of plants), which were imported by the Dutch colonists during the 19th century. In general, sarong *buketan* were multicolored, but this particular blue and white *kain panjang* was created as a Chinese mourning outfit (*kain kelengan*). Moreover, it is decorated in the *pagi–sore* (morning–afternoon) style, with two different patterns on the two halves. The border between the two halves may be diagonal, as here, or vertical. With this type of *kain*, the Javanese have created a very practical garment. In the morning, the dark side is worn on the outside. By turning the *kain* 180 degrees, the light half, which is still clean, can be worn on the outside in the afternoon. (Caption by Annegret Haake)

Batik: Fabled Cloth of Java
Inger McCabe Elliott

For much of my professional life I saw the world in black and white. Buddhists and Catholics killing each other in the streets of Saigon—black and white. Ulanova and Plisetskaya in performance at the Bolshoi Ballet—black and white. Marlon Brando on a Mekong steamer—black and white. Lithuanian survivors of World War II—black and white. I was a photojournalist and those were my primary colors.

Then one day my black and white world exploded into glorious color. It happened in a tiny, nondescript shop in Hong Kong, that moment when the splendors of Java's north coast batik burst upon me. It was an epiphany of sorts, the revelation of a textile cosmos where lions ferociously roar, ducks serenely paddle, mythical animals defy gravity and surreal flowers unfurl their brilliant petals. The batik artists of Java's north coast splashed their colors with uncontrolled abandon.

Entranced by what I first glimpsed in that Hong Kong shop, I set out to unravel the mystery of batik. Before long, I was traveling the length of coastal Java working with local Javanese, Chinese and Arab batik artists, helping them design new patterns, rearranging old ones, mixing colors never before used in batik and demonstrating that it was possible to produce batik in lengths of 32 yards, long enough to be used not just for clothing but for upholstery and drapery as well. Later, my company China Seas Inc. helped open new markets for batik in Europe, the US, Asia and even Latin America.

At first timidly, and then with increasing confidence, I began buying batik that seemed unusual. I used my eyes. Did a particular batik resemble another in color, design and technique? Chances were that they both came from the same region, the same town, the same period and, quite likely, the same artist.

During this long and often arduous search, I traveled to four continents, crawled through cobwebbed attics, slogged through slithering mud and battled flying cockroaches. I was apprehended by armed police when I arrived unannounced at a remote village. I pestered scholars and friends alike in the hope of collecting and showing what had never been seen before, drawing on my training as an aspiring historian. Gradually, I put most of the textiles into what seemed to me to be an appropriate cultural, geographic and historic context.

Java has been at a crossroads of trade for hundreds of years thanks to its location near routes sailed by Marco Polo, Ferdinand Magellan, Sir Francis Drake and St Francis Xavier. Trade brought with it a succession of religions and waves of colonization. Indonesia's motto, "Unity in Diversity", easily describes the wonders of its cloth. The predominant religion is Islam, while its architecture is a mixture of Dutch colonial and petrodollar kitsch, its middle class is Chinese and its lingua franca is Bahasa Indonesia. Each of these influences can be found in the many-splendored batik of Java's north coast.

Batik: Fabled Cloth of Java was conceived more than five decades ago from many collections, including my own. The book served as the catalogue for a major exhibit that was the brainchild of Mattiebelle Gittinger of the Textile Museum in Washington. From the nation's capital, the exhibition traveled to the Royal Ontario Museum in Canada, the Cooper-Hewitt in New York City and the Sewall Museum in Houston, introducing the wondrous colors and forms of north coast batik to a wider audience.

That book and exhibit were the impetus for curating my own collection of about 750 Southeast Asian textiles—complete with detailed descriptions and photographs—that I subsequently donated to the Los Angeles County Museum of Art. In 1996, the museum produced an exhibit of my collection that also traveled to the Cleveland Museum of

Art. *Fabric of Enchantment: Batik from the North Coast of Java*, written by Harmen C. Veldhuisen and Rens Heringa, accompanied the exhibit.

Organizing and cataloguing materials for a book on batik was no easy task. Textiles are notoriously difficult to preserve, especially in the tropics. Mary Hunt Kahlenburg, a knowledgeable textile connoisseur, showed three woven, carbon-dated cloths from the 15th and 16th centuries. I unfortunately didn't find any extant batik created before 1800.

The first person to write authoritatively on batik was Sir Thomas Stamford Raffles, the founder of Singapore and source of the city-state's eponymous hotel, who spent five years in what was known as the East Indies before producing his history in 1817. More than fifty years later, E. van Rijckoversel, a Dutchman, spent four years in Java and collected batik that he donated to the Rotterdam Museum. By 1883, batik was shown in a colonial exhibit in Amsterdam, and fifteen years later, another show in The Hague spurred further interest. That show bore the curious title *Colonial Women's Labor* (Koloniale Frauenarbeit). A monograph by G. P. Rouffaer and Dr H. H. Juynboll appeared in 1900, and six years later the Dutch colonial government assigned S. M. Pleyte and J. E. Jasper to do a further study of folk art, including batik. These four men provided the cornerstone for all subsequent Javanese batik scholarship.

Indonesia's multifaceted batik designs can be traced to the nation's volatile neighbors as well as its own chaotic history. Hindu, Buddhist, Muslim and colonial cultures all contributed to the cacophony of form and color. In modern times, President Sukarno promulgated the slogan "Batik Indonesia" in an attempt to create an autonomous textile business.

Other leaders, including President Suharto and his wife, continued the tradition. But times and customs have changed. When I first visited the north coast in 1970, almost every man, woman and child wore a sarong. This is no longer the case, except perhaps on highly festive occasions. Nowadays, after half a century of tumultuous politics, corruption, greed, overpopulation and recent attempts by militant groups to form a fundamentalist Muslim state, batik is considered an art form.

About the Author

Inger McCabe Elliott, who lives in New York City, was born in Norway and has lived and worked around the world. She graduated from Cornell University with Honors in History and then completed a Masters degree at Harvard in Government and History. Despite an academic background, she has always focused on the arts.

Inger Elliott's photographic career covers half a century, including years as a member of the distinguished photographic agency Rapho-Guillumette. Her work has appeared in *Life*, *Esquire*, *Newsweek*, the *New York Times*, the *Yale Review* and many other international publications. Assignments have included riots in Saigon, Chinese refugees, films and cityscapes as diverse as Houston, Hong Kong and Lhasa. Her prints are in MOMA's permanent collection. She has also written and photographed three books for children.

In her role as founder and president of China Seas, Inc., Inger Elliott wrote and photographed *Batik: Fabled Cloth of Java*. Her curated textiles were donated and exhibited at the Los Angeles County Museum of Art and at the Cleveland Museum of Art, the Textile Museum and the Royal Ontario Museum. She is also the author of *Exteriors*, a work exploring how color informs shapes and textures.

As a consultant to Sotheby's, Inger Elliott helped the auction house redefine its client base, identifying trends in buying and selling art. She also established a highly successful (and copied) series, "Conversations at Sotheby's", that explored the creative process from the perils of politics to art and theater, diplomacy, music and film.

A Prophetic Gift
Brigitte Khan Majlis

For decades, one of my drawers has "housed" a small *canting* with a copper spout and a wooden handle that is perfectly comfortable to hold. Whenever the instrument catches my eye, it brings to mind two people who are closely linked to my passion for textiles.

During the 1970s, master weaver Irmgard Timmermann lectured at the Department of Cultural and Social Anthropology of the University of Cologne. She unlocked the secrets of textile techniques for a large number of students, and many were fired with enthusiasm for this field by her teaching, which involved a rich selection of objects. It was during one of those events at the old Rautenstrauch-Joest Museum (RJM) building on Ubierring that I met Rudolf Smend. We entered into a conversation, and when we next met he gave me the *canting* mentioned above, which has been part of my small textile collection ever since. At that time, I would never have dreamt that the field of Indonesian textiles and, consequently, batik would come to play such an important role in my life. Rudolf's intuition was obviously better developed than mine.

After graduating from university, I had the good fortune of working on several temporary projects at the Rautenstrauch-Joest Museum and of being appointed the curator of its textile department in 1993. In the early 1980s, I conducted a research project on the collections of Indonesian textiles kept in the museums of North Rhine-Westphalia, initiated by the former RJM director and textile enthusiast Professor Gisela Völger.

This renewed my contact with Rudolf Smend, who had made a name for himself with his batik gallery in the so-called "Südstadt" of Cologne, very close to the museum. He showed and explained to me the treasures in his batik collection, training my inexperienced eye. This allowed me to begin to appreciate the range and quality of the batik in the RJM, the Deutsches Textilmuseum in Krefeld and the Von der Heydt-Museum in Wuppertal. Moreover, Rudolf introduced me to Alit Veldhuisen-Djajasoebrata and Harmen Veldhuisen, veterans of batik research to whom I am indebted for the wealth of information they shared with me.

Another person I met through Rudolf was Don Harper, then a dealer and collector of Indonesian textiles in Yogyakarta. Thus, my research project gave rise to a network of Indonesian textile aficionados that has continued to this day. At that time, our findings were included in a catalogue, *Indonesische Textilien: Wege zu Göttern und Ahnen* (Indonesian Textiles: Paths to Gods and Ancestors) and two exhibitions held in parallel at the RJM in Cologne and the Deutsches Textilmuseum in Krefeld in 1984–5. The openings were attended by His Highness Hamengku Buwono IX, the then Sultan of Yogyakarta, and his wife.

That exhibition on Indonesian textiles brought the RJM to the attention of collectors and sponsors devoted to the same subject. In the years and decades that followed, the museum received hundreds of textiles in donations, but it also increased its holdings through specific purchases which, in the case of batik, almost exclusively stemmed from Galerie Smend's stock.

Before 1984, the RJM held just 39 batik cloths, one of them a sarong from Lasem acquired by Wilhelm Joest during his journey in Asia in 1883. Now the museum owns 139 pieces of batik, including several important collections. Hans Wilhelm Siegel, collector of East Asian art, willed to the museum 40 precious batik textiles of varying provenance. Collector Richard Chatwick came to the museum via Rudolf Smend's gallery. Generous sponsorship from another textile collector in Hanover allowed us to acquire 35 batik items assembled by Chatwick over many years. In the main, they are Central Javanese batik cloths, which optimized our textile holdings from that region.

In 2000, the RJM's focus was again on Indonesian textiles, this time including almost 70 batik cloths from the Rudolf Smend Collection. The event was preceded by several weeks in which Rudolf, my colleague Dr Jutta Engelhard (Head of the Indonesia Department and Deputy Director) and myself inspected, discussed, admired, touched and pored over hundreds of batik fabrics in order to eventually, and with great reluctance, make a selection. We would have loved to display them all. Again, a high-profile guest was present—His Highness Sultan Hamengku Buwono X of Yogyakarta.

In the autumn of that same year, Dr Engelhard and I had the opportunity of visiting the Sultan of Yogyakarta and viewing parts of his batik collection. It included several *kain panjang* made by his mother. During the visit, I was fascinated to observe a group of palace ladies, advanced in years, who were applying wax resist for batik in the shade of a *pendopo* (open-sided pavilion). They all wore *kain panjang* in colors and designs that testified to their connection with the palace. In a concentrated and apparently effortless way, they used the *canting* to draw the lines or to apply tiny wax dots, intermittently blowing into the fine

spouts to facilitate the flow of the wax. My eyes were opened to a new aspect of the craft, that of the devotion, time and traditional knowledge that go into creating batik.

When setting up the permanent exhibition in the new RJM building in 2010, batik from Java was given a special position in the "Status" department dedicated to clothing and adornment. The cloths are displayed in a cabinet to illustrate the way in which regional provenance is expressed by means of special textiles. In a display entitled *Gezeichnete Botschaften: Batikkleidung aus Java, Westindonesien* (Messages in Patterns: Batik Clothing from Java, West Indonesia), we show the various ways in which different regional characteristics developed in Java as a result of varying conditions and needs, both in appearance and in the use of the textiles. While the batik made in the north coast port towns indicates ethnicity, Central Javanese designs and colors are guided by the traditions of the Islamic sultans' courts, reflecting the wearers' social status. We owe the success of our eye-catching display to Rudolf Smend's expertise. For our reopening, I was able to select a number of his high-quality batik cloths, which are perfectly suited to the themes we are concerned with. It was the culmination of a connection that began with the prophetic gift of a *canting*, and was strengthened over several decades by our shared enthusiasm for Indonesian textiles.

About the Author
Brigitte Khan Majlis is curator of the Textile Department at the Rautenstrauch-Joest Museum—Cultures of the World, Cologne, Germany.

Chance, Fate or Magic?
Rudolf Smend

Chance or fate, providence or good planning, a friendly spirit or magic?

If it had not been for the jellyfish in the sea at Batu Ferringhi, I would not have come across batik and Chuah Thean Teng in Penang in Malaysia in January 1973.

If it had not been for my visit to Yogyakarta Zoo, I would probably never have met Bambang Oetoro.

If it had not been for Ardiyanto, the amateur hairdresser, I would probably not have encountered antique batik.

If it had not been for Iwan Tirta's money troubles, I would never have been able to purchase a *dodot* (a long ceremonial cloth).

And if it had not been for my visit to the Pasar Beringharjo of Yogyakarta, I would probably not have met Donald Harper.

What if? And what do these events and encounters have to do with my life, with my profession? Many a time, things are easier to explain with hindsight, and a curriculum vitae appears straightforward. But one of life's lessons is that this is not the case.

In 1972, I was one of those whom Brigitte Khan Majlis described in one of her contributions, *The Art of Indonesian Textiles*, p. 9: "… in the 1970s enthusiastic young travelers in search of enlightenment and adventure arrived in the archipelago. Some of them stayed on, some of them went back, but most of them had fallen in love with the textiles they encountered." But it would be a long journey before I arrived at my love affair with batik. Chance set the ball rolling, chance in the shape of a jellyfish that clung so tightly to my arm when I was bathing on a northern beach in Penang that I decided I had better visit the hospital in Georgetown. Rather than continue on my travels, I was forced to stay for three days of treatment. I was told to rest and, as a result, discovered the Batik Art Gallery near the hospital run by Chua Thean Teng and his sons. As a souvenir of their hospitality, I purchased a batik cloth. It was both beautiful and easy to carry in my backpack.

Heavy items were out of the question. After all, my girlfriend and I were traveling overland from Germany to Australia. It was not until I unpacked my backpack in Bali many months later that I came across the batik cloth again. By that time, however, we had already decided to open a batik gallery in Cologne.

What prompted this sudden change of heart? What made us abandon our plan of emigrating to Australia and to return to Germany instead? One of the pieces of the jigsaw was definitely our visit to the Yogyakarta Zoo.

As was usual in those days, we would sometimes set out on bicycles, and a ride to the zoo was recommended, especially a visit to the monkey enclosures after one had had a smoke. However, it was the monsoon season and we were caught in a downpour so heavy that we needed to find a place to take shelter. This happened to be Bambang Oetoro's batik gallery. Although we had seen the name in the *APA Guide to Java*, the subject of batik meant little to us at the time. It kept on raining, and to continue our bicycle ride was out of the question. We thus spent many hours in the studio and exhibition rooms of Bambang's gallery. We had plenty of time to browse through the guest books on display, which were filled with friendly comments from international visitors. A feature in the arts section of a German newspaper caught my eye. One of Bambang Oetoro's students, Hellmut Urban, had organized a batik exhibition at a bank in southern Germany. What a brilliant idea—to combine art and commerce, strengthen the friendship between the nations of Indonesia and Germany and draw attention to an exotic technique among the run-of-the-mill arts and crafts businesses.

Suddenly we had a vision, even a plan. "We will buy tasty Teh Gopek, stock up on cheap batik, open a tea shop in Germany and decorate the walls with Javanese batik." The plan was simple enough. Batik was selling from between two and ten dollars in the young batik artists' studios in the Taman Sari area, and fifty pieces would be sufficient to assemble an exhibition. Moreover, we were lucky enough to find a sponsor in Ardiyanto Pranata. He had faith in our idea and let us take the batik we wanted on a commission basis.

Back in Germany, we quickly realized that no one except us was keen on drinking Gopek tea. Our idea was years ahead of its time. However, we had picked the right moment for introducing exotic cloths from faraway Indonesia, although back in Bali we had no inkling of this. The batik attracted buyers, initially at market stalls and later at the art fairs held in Basel, Düsseldorf and Cologne. We had made a start, embarking on a journey that would last over forty years. The history of our gallery, and its many ups and downs, is too long to describe in detail here. However, a number of events should be mentioned in this context and in this article.

In the mid-1970s, I visited Ardiyanto in his gallery on Jalan Malioboro in order to settle the commission on his goods and get a haircut. Apart from being a geologist, an artist and a collector of stones, he was also adept at wielding a pair of hairdressing scissors. As Ardiyanto was cutting my hair, another visitor arrived with a bundle of fabrics he wished to show him. They were fabrics of a kind I had never seen before.

Ardiyanto and his visitor conversed in the local language. I did not understand a word, but I immediately realized that something was wrong. Ardiyanto had become very agitated. He went to a cabinet to take out some textiles. What had happened? His collection of antique batik had been stolen and by a circuitous route some of those pieces were now being offered to him again. Naturally, this led to an angry exchange in the shop.

Later, Ardiyanto explained to me what had happened. He showed me batik bearing the signatures E. van Zuylen, Jans, The Tie Siet et al. They opened a whole new world to me. I had

never seen antique batik before. They were even more beautiful than the new batik! Ardiyanto became my teacher.

Back in Europe, I searched for literature on the subject but did not find very much except for some beautiful old books by Mas Pirngadie and Rouffaer published in the 1920s and earlier.

However, I was in luck as Alit Veldhuisen-Djajasoebrata, the curator of Indonesian textiles at the Rotterdam Museum of Ethnology, had just published her book *Batik op Java*. We arranged to meet. At the Museum of Ethnology I was able to view cabinets several meters in length, their drawers filled with carefully rolled-up batik. I was overwhelmed. Such beauty, such extraordinary variety and such quantity!

On one of my next trips to Jakarta, I visited the gallery on Jalan Pekalongan run by Iwan Tirta. We knew each other from the days when he presented a breathtaking batik fashion show in Cologne. He was pleased to see me again and indicated that there were a couple of matters he wanted to discuss with me. The first was that he was in urgent need of money to pay his workers. That was something I could help with. He sold me a splendid *dodot* with gold leaf and his workers were paid their money.

The second matter needed more time. He revealed that he was planning to sell his batik collection to a museum. He gave me all the documents pertaining to his batik collection to take home and present to the director of the Deutsches Textilmuseum in Krefeld. So many beautiful and rare designs! I was excited and managed to inspire the same enthusiasm in Carl-Wolfgang Schümann, the museum's director.

Although the city of Krefeld was unable to raise the funds for purchasing the collection, Iwan's mission allowed me to acquire a great deal of information about batik. Irwan's collection has now found a very worthy home in Canberra, in the National Gallery of Australia, and is on view on the museum's website.

Another significant encounter took place at the Pasar Beringharjo in Yogyakarta. Guidebooks recommend this market because of its size and huge range of goods. As cultured travelers, we also like to tick off the sights on our list. But, like many men, I am shopophobic. But like it or not, I did make it to the market. I was strolling aimlessly along the dark and densely crowded passages when I suddenly spotted three women sitting at the back, surrouded by piles of batik cloths. I had expected to find vegetables and spices, not batik! The fabrics were second-hand pieces, and as such they appealed to me even more than new ones. I decided to have a shirt tailored and began to look for a suitable piece 2.5 meters long. My search went on for some time because the selection was breathtaking. The women were mistresses of their trade, outdoing each other and constantly pulling out new pieces for me to see.

I was completely overwhelmed and unable to make a decision. It was dark and hot and I was thirsty. Suddenly, all I wanted to do was get out of the place. At that moment, another foreigner joined us and was enthusiastically greeted by the three women with "Hello Mista Don". I was happy to let him go ahead of me and watched him as they conversed. He was fluent in the local language. They laughed together and suddenly the mood changed to a very pleasant and relaxed atmosphere that extended to me as well. Who was that man? Why was everyone so warm and friendly towards him? And how did he decide which fabrics to select? What was his criteria? He went through all the piles of batik, piece by piece. He was obviously an expert, probably a buyer for a large foreign company. I overcame my reserve, introduced myself and invited him to have a sunset drink at the food stall across from the market. It was the beginning of my wonderful friendship with Donald Harper.

The history of the years that followed can be outlined in brief. Our batik gallery opened in Cologne in June 1973, and is still at the same address in Mainzer Straße.

Many batik exhibitions followed, initially involving artists from Java—Gianto, Tulus Warsito, Harjiman Mashar, An. Sujanto, Ardiyanto, Sunaryo, Wishnu and many others. All of them passed on their expertise in the batik courses held at the gallery. Later we held international batik exhibitions featuring artists as renowned as Noel Dyrenforth, Fritz Donart, Jonathan Evans, Peter Wenger, Susanne Dölker, Joachim Blank and Shouko Kobayashi, to name a few.

We also exhibited the work of those artists in the land of batik itself, at the Taman Ismail Marzuki (TIM) in Jakarta, the Goethe-Institute in Bandung and Gadjah Mada University in Yogyakarta.

We self-published various publications on the themes of batik and painting on silk. Our additional involvement in silk painting and our many training courses meant that our gallery thrived from the mid-1980s. This was essential because by that time Karin and I had got married and our children, Kerstin and Simon, were old enough to go to school.

My publication *Batik: Javanese and Sumatran Batiks from Courts and Palaces* was launched at a batik exhibition held at the Cologne Rautenstrauch-Joest Museum in 2000. His Highness Sultan Hamengku Buwono X traveled to the event from Yogyakarta, together with his wife Queen Hamas, to open the exhibition.

In 2006, the City of Krefeld invited us to display part of our batik collection at the Deutsches Textilmuseum to mark the 100th anniversary of the first batik exhibition ever held in Germany, at the Kaiser-Wilhelm-Museum. At that time, in 1906, the Kaiser-Wilhelm-Museum had had to borrow its exhibits from abroad. The batik came from The Hague and belonged to Queen Wilhelmina. The *wayang kulit* were

Pilgrims from Malang and Pasuruan, ca. 1900.

owned by Sri Susuhunan Pakubuwono X of Surakarta, Central Java. A hundred years after that first exhibition in Germany, a telephone call to Cologne was enough to inspire a further exhibition and accompanying publication, *Batik: 75 Selected Masterpieces, The Rudolf G. Smend Collection*.

The current publication gives further recognition to batik. Today, there is a danger that the old techniques of batik-making may disap-

pear, but thankfully people in Java are aware of the need to preserve this cultural heritage. However, the artistic skill that created the batik illustrated in this book has been irrevocably consigned to the past. All that is left to our generation is to bow our heads in gratitude to the many nameless designers, craftswomen and dyers whose imagination, endurance and skill have allowed us to derive so much pleasure from these wonderful fabrics.

Back to His Roots
Antje Soléau
Forty years of Galerie Smend in Cologne

When Rudolf Smend opened his batik gallery in the southern part of Cologne on 20 June 1973, most people in the gallery business thought he was eccentric, to put it mildly. Not one of them believed that his gallery would survive longer than a year. Now that year has become 480 months and looks set to continue well into the future. The large art galleries, on the other hand, some of them world famous, have all but disappeared. Rudolf Smend discovered a niche and has used this position shrewdly. He has managed to put his personal enthusiasm for a particular subject, the art of Indonesian batik, to good commercial use.

Unlike countries with an historical connection with Indonesia, such as the Netherlands, batik as an art form for designing textiles was largely unknown in Germany at the time, and only gradually became popular with the advent of the do-it-yourself movement and "flower power". A graduate in business studies, Smend seized the opportunity and offered relevant craft courses in addition to his original Javanese batik. A range of associated materials completed his package. When the batik movement tailed off in the 1980s and silk painting became the rage, he adopted the trend and employed the same recipe for success—exhibitions, courses and art materials. At that point, he added books to his repertoire as there was no precursor to silk painting in Germany and specialist literature therefore did not exist. In 1983, Smend published his first book on silk painting, producing his sixth and last in 1998 for the gallery's 25th anniversary. The heyday of silk painting in Germany was over.

Although Galerie Smend still offers courses, the required accessories and relevant publications, it now faces substantial competition from the online trade. While the gallery employed nine staff in 1998, the number of employees has dwindled to three, one of them being Smend's wife Karin, who has been steadily working in the background as the gallery's stalwart since 1978! The third mainstay of the staff is Mustafa Pulathaneli from Ankara, who joined in 1973. Rudolf Smend met him on his famous overland trip to Australia in 1972 that eventually ended in Indonesia.

In all those years, Rudolf Smend never lost his love for Indonesian batik. Quite to the contrary. Slowly but with unerring instinct, and with the necessary specialist knowledge acquired over the years, he has compiled an exquisite collection of historic Indonesian batik, all made between 1870 and ca. 1925. He purchased his treasures locally, that is, on Java, Sumatra and Bali, in markets, from dealers and from private individuals wishing to divest themselves of inconvenient legacies, as well as from princes' courts and sultans' palaces. His collection has now achieved international renown and museum quality! Consequently, Smend has continued to sell individual objects to various museums. It was almost a matter of course that in 2000 the Cologne Rautenstrauch-Joest Museum, the only museum of ethnography in North Rhine-Westphalia, exhibited a highly successful selection of some fifty hip and breast cloths, head cloths and cloths for carrying children as well as several ritual weavings.

Six years later, in 2006, the Deutsches Textilmuseum in Krefeld staged a commemorative display harking back to the first major exhibition of Indonesian art objects ever shown in Germany, at the Kaiser-Wilhelm-Museum, Krefeld in 1906, presenting 75 selected batiks from the Smend Collection that had never previously been exhibited, much less published. In 2010, Rudolf Smend finally opened his own batik museum a few doors away from his gallery, which is open to visitors upon request at any time during the gallery opening hours. To celebrate the 40th anniversary of his gallery, he will once more unite his contemporary "stars" for a major exhibition featuring artists who have explored batik for many years, even during the heyday of silk painting. They are Els van Baarle, Joachim Blank, Fritz Donart, Noel

Dyrenforth, Kobayashi Shoukoh, Annette Pöllmann and Peter Wenger as well as Rita Trefois, Brigitte Willach, Hélène de Ridder, Monika Speyer, Jacques Coenye, Matti Braun and Jonathan Evans. While the prevalence of male exhibiting artists may be surprising at first glance, the selection is quite obviously in line with the Indonesian tradition, where batik is a male domain. It only became a female domain in Europe, or through Europeans. The exhibition shows that Rudolf Smend has come full circle. He has arrived at his very point of departure—batik.

Since his early days as a gallery owner, Rudolf Smend has regularly attended fairs to promote Indonesian batik in an effort to gain its wider acceptance. Especially in Germany, his colleagues in the art business have made his life difficult. There were occasions when he was obliged to enlist a solicitor to battle for his stand at certain fairs! The major art galleries simply did not wish to acknowledge batik as an art form. They were blinded by the proverbial German rigidity. Rudolf Smend took the logical step of taking his business abroad. To mention just one event, this spring he was represented at the *Textile & Tribal Arts Show* in San Francis-

co. His Krefeld exhibition, or parts of it, has also traveled abroad for shows in Riga, Latvia; Lowell, MA as well as the Polish cities of Łodz, Warsaw and Krakow. The only German venue was the Max-Berk-Textilmuseum in Heidelberg. In the Warsaw and Krakow shows, the exhibits from the Rudolf Smend Collection were juxtaposed with Polish batik. Batik production based on the Javanese model flourished in Poland in the early 20th century and was practised not only on textiles but also on wood and ceramics. Held in 2006 and 2007, each of the two exhibitions was accompanied by a catalogue in Polish and English produced by the respective hosts.

Looking back on Rudolf Smend's career as a gallery owner, publisher and collector of batik, and on his acceptance in the German art scene, the saying about the "prophet who went unheeded in his own country" springs to mind. Only a very few specialist museums, selected artists and collectors take an interest in this highly specialized form of textile art. Rudolf Smend has found a niche in the art trade that has allowed him and his gallery to survive for what is now forty years. Thankfully, the future looks good.

(Contribution to *Textilkunst International*, Vol. 41, No. 2, 2013, pp. 63–6.)

Galerie Smend Publications

1977 *Batik: Europäische Künstler in Südost-Asien* [European Artists in South-East Asia]
1980 *Batik Handbuch* [Batik Handbook]
1983 *Seidenmalerei. Handbuch I* [Painting on Silk. Handbook I]
1984 *Internationale Batik-Ausstellung* [International Batik Exhibition]
1985 *Malerei auf Seide. Handbuch II* [Painting on Silk. Handbook II]
1987 *Seide–Farbe–Seidenmalerei. Handbuch III* [Silk–Color–Silk Painting. Handbook III]
1989 *Seidenmalerei. Handbuch IV* [Painting on Silk. Handbook IV]
1993 *Seidenmalerei. Handbuch V* [Painting on Silk. Handbook V]
1998 *25 Jahre Textile Kunst: Galerie Smend 1973–1998. Handbuch VI* [25 Years of Textile Arts]
2000 *Batik: Javanese and Sumatran Batiks from Courts and Palaces, Rudolf G. Smend Collection*
2006 *Batik: 75 Selected Masterpieces, The Rudolf G. Smend Collection*

Javanese Batik
to the World
Maria Wrońska-Friend

My first acquaintance with Javanese batik took place in 1978 in Łodz, a city in central Poland that used to be known as the Polish Manchester on account of its extensive textile industry. At the time, I was completing a degree in anthropology, and my attention had already been drawn to the richness of the cultural traditions of Southeast Asia. Our student group decided to organize a seminar dedicated to various aspects of Asian cultures, with a local textile factory offering to sponsor the event. My plan was to give a presentation on *wayang* theater, but the organizers insisted that in order to acknowledge the sponsor at least one of the papers should address textiles. "The people of Indonesia make such unusual fabrics decorated with wax…. This is somewhat similar to our Easter egg decorations…. Maybe you could give a presentation on that topic?" Reluctantly I agreed, and thirty-five years later I am still fascinated by the batik of Java and am trying to understand the finer points of the technique and the complex meanings of these fabrics.

My interest in batik provided me with the opportunity to meet several quite exceptional and inspirational people. In the 1980s, I worked for two months in the workshop of the batik master Bambang Oetoro in Yogyakarta, learning the intricacies of wax-drawn patterns. While continuing my studies of batik, I benefited from the advice of two highly respected connoisseurs of these textiles—K. R. T. Hardjonagoro and Iwan Tirta. In Europe, I met several collectors of Indonesian textiles and was particularly privileged to be given access to the extensive collection of Javanese batiks owned by Rudolf Smend in Cologne.

Batik has always been a dynamic, flexible tradition, able to change and respond to new demands, opportunities and challenges. As a result, a multitude of regional and ethnic styles of batik have emerged, with their colors and designs acting as an elaborate system of visual communication. Those who understand this language can, by looking at the fabric, easily identify the person's social position, his or her ethnicity, marital status, age and the occasion on which the cloth is worn.

Of course, I have my personal favorites, one being batik from the Central Javanese palaces with *nitik* (meaning "dot") patterns that are made by carefully applying thousands of wax drops or dashes in a repeated geometric design. Creating *nitik* patterns was almost a meditative practice that required an amazing degree of concentration and patience. These fabrics provide testimony to K. R. T. Hardjonagoro's statement that the genuine function of batik is to calm the disquieted soul.

I also admire batiks that used to be made in the late 19th and early 20th centuries in the small town of Lasem along the north coast of Java in workshops owned by Chinese Peranakan. Among several types of local batik, frequently called *laseman*, the sarongs decorated with the tree of life motif are of particular beauty (see no. 34 page 80, no. 38 page 82, no. 39 page 84 and no. 53 page 106). This is a Javanese rendition of the famous *citta* cloths from the Indian Coromandel Coast, which in previous centuries used to be traded to Indonesia as well as Europe, where in English-speaking countries they became known as chintz. The Lasem version of the tree of life cloth is unique as it combines the paramount floral motif of India with Chinese and Javanese imagery.

The faultless execution of these fabrics testifies to the artistic mastery of the designers responsible for planning and setting up the work, the technical skills of the women who painstakingly drew the complex wax patterns, as well as the expertise of the local dyers who,

Close-up of the Chinese tiger on a pair of batik trousers (*celana*), page 111.

by conducting centuries-long experiments, mastered the art of coloring cotton with plant matter long before the introduction of synthetic dyes.

The iconography of Javanese batik reflects the influence of a multitude of cultural traditions, especially those of India, China, Europe and the Middle East. Few people, however, realize that it was a two-way process. Javanese batik has not only borrowed from the cultural traditions of other countries but its techniques and aesthetics have become an inspiration to textile traditions in other parts of the world. My current mission is to make Indonesian people aware of the importance of their textiles as a source of global inspiration. For example, batik from Java influenced European Art Nouveau and Art Deco and left its mark on the works of artists as well known as Henry van de Velde, Henri Matisse and Charles Rennie Mackintosh. It has also influenced the iconography of the industrial textiles of Africa, the fabrics of Indian West Bengal, where the technique was introduced by Rabindranath Tagore following his visit to Java, and even the textile art of the Aboriginal people of the central desert of Australia. Javanese batik has become a global, transcultural phenomenon, an art form that brings together people living in distant parts of the world.

Growing up With Batik
Haryani Winotosastro

I was born into a family with a strong batik tradition. From my great-grandparents down to my parents, all were involved in either producing batik or trading in it. Drawing on the batik-making skills passed on over four generations, my father established his own batik factory in 1940, starting with just seven workers. The following year, he married my mother, and together they ran the batik factory.

Together with my sister and brothers, I helped in the family business. We studied batik designs, the traditional batik process, the customs related to batik as well as the business of batik. I was fortunate enough to be able to study chemistry at university, which gave me a better understanding of the dyeing process in batik making.

In 1947, my father and several fellow batik producers in Yogyakarta formed a batik co-operative. Later, he became one of the pioneers of Gabungan Koperasi Batik Indonesia (GKBI), the Association of Indonesian Batik Co-operatives. This is an organization that acts as an umbrella for all batik businesses in Indonesia.

My father began to introduce batik internationally in the late 1960s. He traveled to five continents to present batik. I had the chance to accompany him on some of his trips to Europe, Japan and the USA for trade missions or batik exhibitions.

After my parents passed away, I took over the running of the manufacturing plant and maintained the process and knowledge of traditional hand wax batik in medium- and high-quality batik, which I had inherited. Some of our customers are museums and collectors who request renewal of their antique cloth collections before the original ones are destroyed permanently. They also ask my advice on how to store batik fabrics to avoid damage. I am glad that I am able to provide advice, having observed the practices of major museums in other countries.

Another skill I have is batik making in the *tambal* (patchwork) style, where the patches are filled with different motifs (see photos pages 59 and 118). In 2007, I designed a cloth containing classic Yogyakarta batik designs. Symmetry is important in the study of material sciences. The cloth was shown at the European Congress of Crystallography held in Marrakech in 2007 by Annegret Haake, who gave a presentation at the event.

I still care for and continue to preserve our cultural heritage of batik, especially the Yogya designs.

hani@winotosastro.com
www.winotosastro.com

Mudjiono and Mudinah Winotosastro (seated) with their children (left to right) Haryani, Supriharjo, Sugeng Prayitno and Sugiarti, Yogyakarta, 1975. On the wall behind are photographs of President Soeharto and Vice-President Sudarmono.

Opposite Two palace custodians dressed in traditional attire of head cloth (*iket*), tunic and sarong, greet each other in a courtyard of the Yogyakarta *kraton*, ca. 1930s.

Contributors' Publications

Annegret Haake
haake.xx-tex@t-online.de

1984   *Javanische Batik: Methode, Symbolik, Geschichte*, M. & H. Schaper, Hanover.

1989   "The Role of Symmetry in Javanese Batik Patterns", in Istvan Hargittai (ed.), *Symmetry: Unifying Human Understanding, II*, Special Issue of Computers & Mathematics with Applications, Pergamon Press, Oxford, Vol. 17, Nos. 1–6, pp. 815–26.

2006   "Die Ursprünge von Patchwork und Quilt: Ihre Besondere Bedeutung in der Javanischen Batik" (The Origins of Patchwork and Quilt: Their Special Meaning in Javanese Batik), *Textilkunst International*, Schaper, Hanover, Vol. 34, No. 3, pp. 143–6.

2009   A. Haake & H. Winotosastro, "Teaching Symmetry: Using Ancient Javanese Batik Patterns", in *Symmetry: Culture and Science*, Symmetrion, Budapest, Vol. 20, Nos. 1–4, pp. 145–60.

2009   "Echte Batik aus Java: Wie unterscheidet man sie von Plagiaten?" (Genuine Batiks from Java: How Can They Be Distinguished from Fakes?), *Textilkunst International*, Schaper, Hanover, Vol. 37, No. 3, pp. 118–24.

2012   "Semen–Batiken–Darstellungen des Javanischen Kosmos" (Semen–Batiks–Presentations of the Javanese Cosmos), *Textilkunst International*, Schaper, Hanover, Vol. 40, No. 4, pp. 195–200.

Donald Harper
batikman@hotmail.com
www.eastindiesmuseum.com

2000   "Collecting Batik in Java", in R. G. Smend (ed.), *Batik: Javanese and Sumatran Batiks from Courts and Palaces, Rudolf G. Smend Collection*, Galerie Smend, Cologne, pp. 81–3.

2006   Interview with Rudolf G. Smend and Donald J. Harper, in R. G. Smend (ed.), *Batik: 75 Selected Masterpieces, The Rudolf G. Smend Collection*, Galerie Smend, Cologne, pp. 146–61.

Jonathan Hope

jonathan.glenhope@virginmedia.com

2008   "Batik Kemben from Surakarta", *Hali*, London, No. 155, pp. 50–1.
2008   Profile about Rudolf Smend, review of his shows, *Hali*, London, No. 157, pp. 34–5.
2009   "Goddess Fish in a Fragrant Garden", *Hali*, London, No. 160, pp. 23–5.
2011   "Cabinet of Curiosities," on the reopened Rautenstrauch-Joest Museum, Cologne, *Hali*, London, No.167, pp. 76–9.
2011   "A Hidden Strength", *Hali*, London, No.168, pp. 45–51.

Inger McCabe Elliott

ingerelliott@gmail.com

1984   *Batik: Fabled Cloth of Java*, Clarkson N. Potter, New York.
1984–5 Exhibition films and posters supported by the Mobil Corporation; reissued with a new cover in the United Kingdom by Viking Press.
1993   *Exteriors*, Clarkson Potter, New York.
2004   *Batik: Fabled Cloth of Java*, re-edited edition, Periplus Editions, Singapore; reissued in paperback, 2006.

Brigitte Khan Majlis
brigitte.majlis@stadt-koeln.de

1984   *Indonesische Textilien: Wege zu Göttern und Ahnen* (Indonesian
        Textiles: Paths to Gods and Ancestors), exhibition catalogue,
        Cologne.
1991   "New Acquisitions in Krefeld and Cologne", in Gisela Völger and
        Karen von Welck (eds.), *Indonesian Textiles*, symposium
        proceedings, Cologne, 1985.
1991   *Gewebte Botschaften: Indonesische Traditionen im Wandel,*
        Woven Messages: Indonesian Textile Tradition in Course of Time,
        exhibition catalogue, Hildesheim.
2000   "Javanese Batik: An Introduction", in R. G. Smend (ed.), *Batik:*
        Javanese and Sumatran Batiks from Courts and Palaces, Rudolf G.
        Smend Collection, Galerie Smend, Cologne, pp. 13–19.
2007   *The Art of Indonesian Textiles: The E. M. Bakwin Collection at the*
        Art Institute of Chicago, exhibition catalogue.
2010   "The Body as a Stage: Clothing and Adornment", in Jutta Engel-
        hard and Klaus Schneider (eds.), *People in Their Worlds:*
        Rautenstrauch-Joest Museum: Cultures of the World, exhibition
        catalogue, Cologne, pp. 140–79.
2011   "Tangled in Time", review of the exhibition "Heirlooms", *Hali*,
        London, No. 170, pp. 122–3.

Rudolf Smend
rudolf@smend.de

2011   "Preserving an Ancient Craft: The Art of Batik", Tribal & Textile
        Arts Show, 10–13 February, San Francisco.
2012   "Batik: A Personal Reflection", *Textile Forum*, Hanover, No. 1,
        pp. 30–7.
2012   "Batik: Eine persönliche Betrachtung", *Kita* (Das Magazin der
        Deutsch-Indonesischen Gesellschaft), Cologne, No. 3, pp. 6–42.
2012   "Magie van de Vrouw", book review, *Textiles Asia Journal,* Hong
        Kong, Vol. 4, No. 2, pp. 25–6.
2014   "Die Batiken des Sultans am Königshof von Siam: Ein
        ungehobener Schatz" (The Sultan's Batiks at the Court of Siam:
        A Hidden Treasure), Thailand Rundschau der Deutsch-
        Thailändischen Gesellschaft, Cologne, Vol. 27, No. 2, pp. 65–7.
2014   "Ein Rock ohne Knopf und Reißverschluss: Der Batik-Sarong"
        (A Skirt Without Buttons or Zips: The Batik Sarong), *Textilgestal-*
        tung (Informationen für den Unterricht), Essen, No. 1, pp. 11–15.

Maria Wrońska-Friend

2000   "Parang Rusak Design in European Art", in M. Hitchcock and
        W. Nuryanti (eds.), *Building on Batik: The Globalization of a Craft
        Community*, University of North London, Ashgate, pp. 109–17.
2001   "Javanese Batiks for European Artists: Experiments at the
        Koloni aal Laboratorium in Haarlem", in Itie van Hout (ed.), *Batik:
        Drawn in Wax, 200 Years of Batik Art from Indonesia*, exhibition
        catalogue, Royal Tropical Institute, Amsterdam, pp. 106–23.
2006   "Javanese Batik: The Art of Wax Design", in R. G. Smend (ed.),
        Batik: 75 Selected Masterpieces, The Rudolf G. Smend Collection,
        Galerie Smend, Cologne, pp. 30–57.
2008   *Sztuka Woskiem Pisana: Batik w Indonezji I Polsce* (Art Drawn
        with Wax: Batik in Indonesia and Poland), Gondwana Publishing,
        Warsaw.
2010   "Batik Dress of Java", in J. Dhamija (ed.) *South and South East Asia*,
        Vol. 4 of J. B. Eicher (ed.), *The Berg Encyclopedia of World Dress
        and Fashion*, J. Berg Publishers, Oxford, pp. 441–7.
2014   "Henry van de Velde and Javanese Batik", in Thomas Föhl and
        Antje Neumann (eds.), *Textiles*, Vol. 2 of *Henry van de Velde:
        Interior Design and Decorative Arts, A Catalogue Raisonné*, 6 vols.,
        Klassik Stiftung Weimar, pp. 371–97.
2015   *Batik bagi Dunia, Javanese Batik to the World*, Lontar, Jakarta.

Overleaf Noble Javanese in the courtyard of the Surakarta
kraton, ca. 1900.

Glossary

Badan The "body" or main field of a sarong that forms the largest area as opposed to the smaller section, the *kepala* or "head".

Banji Chinese swastika motif symbolizing good fortune, used on backgrounds or borders.

Batik Resist-dyed cloth.

Batik cap Block-printed batik.

Batik tulis Hand-drawn batik; a technique where wax is applied using the *canting* tool.

Booh An elaborate bow or scalloped border.

Buketan (from the Dutch *boeket*), 20th-century batik designs with floral bouquets, usually large bouquets arrayed in a line.

Canting Javanese name for a small spouted tool with a copper reservoir used to apply molten wax to the surface of a cloth.

Celana Loose batik trousers.

Chintz (from Hindi), Indian cotton cloth decorated with bright floral patterns.

Cemukiran Flame-like motif found lining diamond and square-shaped centerfields.

Ceplokan Repetitive geometric motifs in a symmetrical arrangement.

Cocohan Thousands of tiny dots drawn on the background of a cloth.

Dlorong Alternating diagonal bands filled with motifs on the *badan* and/or *kepala*.

Dodot Extra large ceremonial court batik made by sewing two *kain panjang* together.

Eurasian *See* Indo-European.

Garuda Mythical bird; the mount of the God Vishnu in Hindu mythology.

Indigo Blue dye obtained from the leaves of the indigo plant (*Indigo tinctoria*).

Indische People of mixed Dutch and Indonesian descent.

Indo-European People of mixed Asian and European ancestry.

Kain An unsewn cloth or skirt cloth.

Kain basurek Lit. "written cloth"; fabric decorated with Arabic inscriptions.

Kain kelengan *See* Kelengan.

Kain laseman Batik made in Lasem with Indian-inspired "tree of life" motifs.

Kain panjang A long skirt cloth.

Kain panjang pagi–sore Lit. "morning–afternoon cloth"; a cloth with two different patterns divided by a diagonal or straight line in the center.

Kain sprei *See* Sprei.

Kawung A famous old Central Javanese motif formed from parallel rows of circles.

Kemben A long narrow cloth wound tightly around a woman's chest.

Kebaya A long-sleeved tailored blouse decorated with lace and embroidery originally worn by Peranakan women with a batik sarong.

Kelengan Blue and white batik traditionally worn during mourning but also by a bride.

Kepala Literally "head". The center or end of a sarong or *kain panjang* design, usually displayed at the front when worn.

Khudung Rectangular cloth worn as a head and shoulder covering by a Muslim woman.

Kraton Javanese palace; royal court.

Laseman *See* Kain laseman.

Latar putih Literally "white background"; a technique in which colored designs appear on a light, undyed background.

Loksan Chinese-inspired real and imaginary motifs generally depicted in lacy patterns on a light background.

Mengkudu A deep red dye obtained from the bark and leaves of *Morinda citrifolia*.

Naga Mythical snake or dragon figure.

Nitik Designs composed of small dots and dashes imitative of weaving or plaiting.

Pagi–sore *See* Kain panjang pagi–sore.

Papan The narrow rectangular bands on the left and right of the broad vertical *kepala*.

Parang A famous Central Javanese "knife" design consisting of alternating light and dark diagonal bands.

Peranakan A native-born person of mixed local and foreign ancestry, e.g. Peranakan Chinese, Peranakan Arabs.

Pesisir Lit. "coast"; towns on the north coast of Java producing a distinctive style of batik in the 19th and 20th centuries.

Pinggir The narrow horizontal borders at the upper and lower edges of a sarong.

Prada Batik decorated on the surface with gold leaf or gold dust.

Sarong Lit. "sheath"; a cloth sewn to form a tubular skirt, always with a *kepala*.

Sarong buketan *See* Buketan.

Sarong dlorong *See* Dlorong.

Sarong kelengan *See* Kelengan.

Sidomukti A composition on the *badan* of a sarong consisting of small motifs enclosed within a latticework.

Sindangan A plain-colored lozenge-shaped centerfield on a *kemben* worn by married women.

Selendang Shoulder cloth.

Soga A brown dye derived from the bark of the soga tree (*Peltophorum ferrugineum*).

Sprei Bed cover.

Tambal A patchwork of Central Javanese motifs set within squares, triangles, circles, etc. in horizontal or slanting rows.

Tanahan Motifs that fill in the backround spaces around the main motifs of a batik.

Tritik A resist dyeing and patterning process involving stitching and gathering cloth before it is dyed.

Tumpal Elongated (isosceles) triangles placed in rows facing each other on the *kepala* of a sarong; half *tumpal* are often placed at the ends of a *kain*.

Wayang Puppets made of leather or wood used in telling stories from the *Ramayana* and *Mahabharata* Hindu epics and other stories; used as a batik motif.

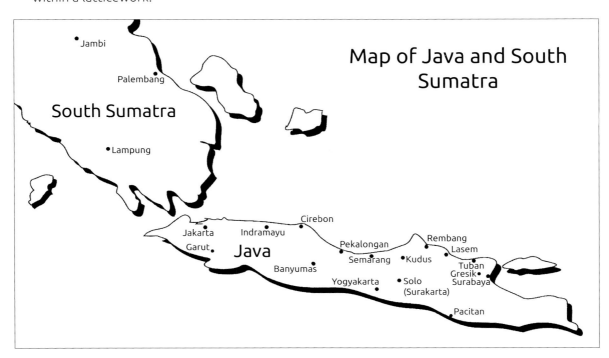

Map of Java and South Sumatra

Select Bibliography*

Achjadi, Judi, "Batik: Java's Gift to the World", *Textiles Asia*, Vol. 3, No. 3, 2012.

_____, *The Glory of Batik: The Danar Hadi Collection*, Batik Danar Hadi, Surakarta, 2011.

Avé, Joop (ed.), *Grand Batik Interiors*, Bab Publishing Indonesia, Jakarta, 2007.

Barnes, Ruth, "Textiles in the Department of Indo-Pacific Art, Yale University Art Gallery", *Textiles Asia*, Vol. 6, No. 1, 2014.

Barnes, Ruth, and Mary Hunt Kahlenberg (eds.), *Five Centuries of Indonesian Textiles: The Mary Hunt Kahlenberg Collection*, DelMonico Books–Prestel, Munich, New York, London, 2010.

Chong, Alan, et al. (eds.), *Devotion and Desire: Cross-Cultural Art in Asia, New Acquisitions of the Asian Civilisations Museum*, Singapore, 2013.

Cutsem-Vanderstraete, Anne van, et al., *Magie van de Vrouw: Magic of Women, Textiles and Jewelry from Indonesia*, Stichting Wereldmuseum, Rotterdam, 2012.

Damais, Asmoro, *Wastra Batik Karya Hardjonagoro Go Tik Swan, 1956–1966*, Buku Katalogus Pameran, Jakarta, 2009.

Haake, Annegret, *Batik Jawa: Metode, Simbolik, Sejarah, Balai Besar Kerajinan Batik Yogyakarta*, Yogyakarta, 2015.

Heringa, Rens, *Nini Towok's Spinning Wheel: Cloth and the Cycle of Life in Kerek, Java*, Fowler Museum at UCLA, Los Angeles, 2010.

Hoopen, Peter ten, *Woven Languages: Indonesian Ikat Textiles from the Peter ten Hoopen Collection*, Museo do Oriente exhibition catalogue, Fundaçao Oriente, Lisbon, 2014.

Ishwara, Helen; L. R. Supriyapto Yahya; Xenia Moeis; Hartono Sumarsono, *Benang Raja: Menyimpul Keelokan Batik Pesisir*, Jakarta, 2013.

_____, *Batik Pesisir Pusaka Indonesia: Koleksi Hartono Sumarsono*, Gramedia, Jakarta, 2011.

Iskandar, Neneng, *Batik Indonesia dan Sang Empu: Go Tik Swan Panembahan Hardjonagoro*, Tim Buku Srihana, Jakarta, 2008.

Knight-Achjadi, Judith, and Asmoro Damais, *Butterflies and Phoenixes: Chinese Inspirations in Indonesian Textile Arts*, Mitra Museum Indonesia, Jakarta, 2005.

Lee, Chor Lin, *Batik: Creating an Identity*, National Museum of Singapore and Editions Didier Millet, Singapore, 2007.

Lee, Peter, *Sarong Kebaya: Peranakan Fashion in an Interconnected World 1500–1950*, Asian Civilisations Museum, Singapore, 2014.

Majlis, Brigitte Khan, *The Art of Indonesian Textiles: The E. M. Bakwin Collection at the Art Institute of Chicago*, New Haven, 2007.

Newton, Gael, *Garden of the East: Photography in Indonesia 1850s–1940s*, National Gallery of Australia, Canberra, 2014.

Pradito, Didit; Herman Jusuf; S. Ken Atik, *The Dancing Peacock: Colours and Motifs of Priangan Batik*, Gramedia, Jakarta, 2010.

*Only titles published post-2005

Ramelan, Tumbu, *The 20th Century Batik Masterpieces: Tumbu Ramelan Collections*, KR Communications, Jakarta, 2010.

Smend, Rudolf G. (ed.), *Batik: 75 Selected Masterpieces, The Rudolf G. Smend Collection*, Galerie Smend, Cologne, 2006.

Sumarsono, Hartono; Helen Ishwara; L. R. Supriyapto Yahya; Xenia Moeis, *Batik Pesisir: An Indonesian Heritage,* Gramedia, Jakarta, 2012.

Tozu, Masakatsu, *All About Batik: Art of Tradition and Harmony*, Machida City Museum, 2007.

Trefois, Rita, *Fascinating Batik; Fascinerend Batik; Le Batik Fascinant*, Ghent, 2009.

Willach, Brigitte, *Highlights from the North Coast to Bima Sakti*, exhibition catalogue, Museum Tekstil Jakarta, Yogyakarta, 2015.

Wrońska-Friend, Maria, *Batik Jawa bagi Dunia: Javanese Batik to the World*, Lontar, Jakarta, 2015.

_____, "Batik of Pasisir: A Symphony of Colours and Patterns", in Christianto Dadang et al., *Batik of Java: Politics and Poetics,* Caloundra Regional Art Gallery, Caloundra, Australia, 2010.

_____, *Sztuka Woskiem Pisana: Batik Indonezji I Polsce* (Art Drawn with Wax: Batik in Indonesia and Poland), Gondwana Publishing, Warsaw, 2008.

_____, *Textiles for Gods and People from the Krzyzstof Musiał Balinese Art Collection*, Central Museum of Textiles, Łodz, 2015.

Yudhoyono, Ani Bambang, *Batikku: Pengabdian Cinta tak Berkata*, Gramedia, Jakarta, 2010.

_____, *My Batik Story: A Silent Labor of Love*, Gramedia, Jakarta, 2010.

Yunus, Noor Azlina, *Malaysian Batik: Reinventing a Tradition*, Tuttle Publishing, Singapore, 2011.

Acknowledgments

Annegret Haake
Antje Soléau
Bill Caskey †
Bonnie Corwin
Brigitte Khan Majlis
Brigitte Willach
Cinta † and Ardiyanto Pranata
Claudius and Gerda Giese
Claus von Zitzewitz †
Constance de Monbrison
Dale C. Gluckman
Daniel Gundlach
Doddy Soepardi
Donald Breyer
Donald Harper, Na Le, Duc, Sana, Baron
Erhard Wesser
Eric Oey
Haryani Winotosastro
Hennie Stolk
Heribert Amann
Ibu Misari
Ibu Munir Darwis
Imelda Akmal
Inger McCabe Elliott
Iwan Tirta †
Jacqueline Simcox
Jan Konietzko
Jonathan Hope
Jörn-Holger Spröde and Kartini
Judo Suwidji
Krysztof Musiał
Leo Haks
Margit Zara Krpata
Maria Wrońska-Friend and Tony Friend
Martin Schalbruch
Mulyadi Utomo
Museum Tekstil (Jakarta Textile Museum)
Nyoman Sukayahadi
Peter Lee
Petra Martin
Smend Family
Sonja Mohr
Susanne Mattern
Thomas Murray
Ulrike Strunden
Wolfgang Thesen

Batik Collections

Claudius Giese
p. 22

Annegret Haake
p. 147

Donald Harper
pp. 46, 48, 64, 66, 100, 101, 102, 103, 104, 105, 106, 107, 122, 124, 128

Rudolf Smend
pp. 12, 14, 16, 18, 20, 24, 26, 28, 30, 32, 34, 36, 38, 40, 42, 44, 50, 54, 68, 70, 72, 74, 76, 78, 79, 80, 81, 82, 84, 86, 88, 90, 92, 94, 96, 98, 108, 109, 111, 112, 126, 127, 130

Mulyadi Utomo
pp. 52–3

Photo Credits

Leo Haks
p. 110: Knife sharpeners. Kassian Céphas, ca. 1890
p. 129: Photographer unknown
p. 155, Pilgrims from Malang and Pasuruan, Dr Christiaan
Snoeck Hurgronje, ca. 1900

Donald Harper
pp. 56, 57, 58, 59, 60, 61, 63, 113, 114, 115, 116, 117, 118,
119, 120, 121, 132, 133, 134, 135, 136, 137, 139, 140, 141,
145
All photographers unknown, with a few exceptions.
All photos from first quarter 20th century.
The people depicted are unknown, with a few exceptions.
Available information:
p. 57: Studio Chelan, Djogja
p. 115: B.R.T. Projodijuro, Djogja
p. 120: Goede mid dag yuffrouw 5-8-26
p. 121: L. Chelan (Studio) 8/9- 27, Djogja (L. Chi Lan)
p. 134: L. Chelan (Studio) 4-8-25 Dk. (Djogjakarta)
p. 139: Gusti Kandjeng Ratu Kentjono sak futro. Djogjakarta
p. 140: Kandjeng Ratu Yu dng, Djogjakarta
p. 141: Poerwokerto, 12-36, di Dieng & Lawet

**Museum für Völkerkunde Dresden (MVD),
Staatliche Kunstsammlungen Dresden (SKD)**
pp. 166–7: "Vornehme Javanen", Palace of Paku Buwono X
(1866–1939), the tenth Susuhunan, Soerakarta, Java,
A. Grubauer, before 1900

Rautenstrauch-Joest Museum, Kulturen der Welt
p. 138: inv. no. 11336, dancers in east Java
p. 161: inv. no. 20313, Yogyakarta Court, ca. 1930

Rudolf Smend
pp. 10–11: An outdoor market in Java, ca. 1890
p. 62: Photographer unknown, first quarter 20th century

Production Credits

Published in conjunction with the exhibition
Batik: Traditional Textiles of Indonesia
From the Rudolf Smend Collection

Galerie Smend
Mainzer Straße 31
50678 Köln, Germany
Fon + 49 (0)221-312047
smend@smend.de
www.smend.de

2 October 2015 (Hari Batik)–30 January 2016

Editor Rudolf Smend, Cologne

Translation German / English
Susanne Mattern, Karben
Maria Schlatter, London

Translation Bahasa Indonesia / German
Kartini and Jörn-Holger Spröde, Jena

Editing
Sonja Mohr, Wuppertal

Layout
Jan Konietzko, Cologne, www.jankonietzko.de

DTP
Ulrike Strunden, Cologne

Photography
Fulvio Zanettini, Cologne, www.zanettini.net
Collection of Donald Harper: Le Thi Na, Saigon

Lenders of Historical Photos
Leo Haks, New Zealand
Donald Harper, Saigon
Museum für Völkerkunde, Dresden
Rautenstrauch-Joest Museum, Cologne
Rudolf Smend, Cologne

Scans
Jan Overduin, Rotterdam, look@coverall.nu

Poem

Text related to batik, pages 22–3
in Ambonese / English

Tabe nona tabe	Farewell, my girl, farewell
saja maoe pigi	I must go
tabe nona tabe	farewell, my girl, farewell
ati saja sedi	my heart is sad
pigi rasa soesa	having to go is hard
nona tingal trada bole	you will stay behind
djangan sampe ati	you must not take it
inget bae bae	too much to heart
kalo saja pigi	remember me fondly
djaoe dari nona	when I go
nona djangan loepa	far away from you
inget kapada saja	don't forget me
djantong ati djiwa	think about me
tida dari saja	my heart and my soul
kalo saja mati	I would not wish
djaoe dari nona	to die
koeboer saja biar nona	far away from you
preksa biken bae bae	may you care well
traoesa siram kembang	for my grave
nona siram aermata sadja	you need not water the flowers
itoe saja trima	simply shed your tears
	that will be enough for me